HOLLOW

HOLLOW

How a Young Man Turned Childhood Trauma Into Music

JAKE PAUL

Jake Paul

CONTENTS

Introduction 2

Part 1: Melodies from Memories

1 The Phone Call 8

2 Hollow 12

3 Providence 23

4 Don't Forget 33

5 Keep Your Demons 46

6 In the End 53

7 Move On 63

CONTENTS

Part 2:

Harmony in Healing: The Tools That Mended My Soul

8 | The Stigma of Being Traumatized   70

9 | Hello Acceptance. Goodbye Anxiety.   78

10 | Synchronicities & Signs   90

Part 3:

Verses of Victory

11 | Statue   99

12 | Go With The Flow   107

13 | My Side of the Street   113

14 | Inhale   120

15 | Inclined   128

| Epilogue   134

Dedication

I dedicate this book to my mother, Chris, who lost her life before I ever got to know who she really was while she was here. I also dedicate this to my dad, "Junior." Thank you for doing the best you could with what you had... and for teaching me how to fish.

I finally see a life full of joy.
You were my hero when I was a boy.

The songs in this book and the stories behind them are more than just lyrics and words. They are deep expressions, reflections, and representations of what I was experiencing at that time in my life. They captured a moment in time, and yet they are time*less*. They mean as much to me today as they did when I wrote them down. When you read them, they may become alive again and ignite something within you too. Like magic spells, they (words) have provided me with the tools to enable change to happen. I wrote down lyrics in order to express deep emotion and those words have manifested into songs, recordings, performances, and now a book - all of which have been the agents of change for me. My hope is that by reading this, you will resonate with my main message: we all have a story of our own to live out, but how we want that story to end is in our hands.

The book title, *Hollow*, is actually the name of a song I wrote about my mother's unexpected death. As you can imagine, that was an extremely difficult time and it impacted many people in and around my family. But the actual trauma I am referring to lies in the wounds that the event caused afterward. You don't have to experience trauma in your life to see the lasting impact it can have on people. It took years of unraveling my own behavior to learn that it is not necessarily the actual event(s) that caused the trauma, but my response to the event. In my case, the news of the actual event was indeed terrifying and traumatic, but it also added elements and layers to other people's behavior that caused even more trauma for me. Further, the case regarding her death was never really solved due to a variety of *situations*, all of which stripped the possibility of closure, in the usual sense, to occur. So a few years back, I ventured to the Muskego Police Department and picked up a copy of the 80 page police report to learn more about the events leading up to her death and how the police and detectives handled it afterward. I wanted to get a clearer, more level-headed perspective on what events really happened according to the police, detectives, and witnesses regarding their experience with this tragic event. After reading the report through and through, I believe I know what actually went down that evening, but I'll never really know for sure. I know she died from a gunshot wound to her chest, which I believe to be a homicide. Like I said, the case was never officially solved though, and although the man who shot her lived, the case never went to court and he was never convicted. A **hollow** feeling inside about it all is where this book (and the song) stems from.

The remainder of the book consists of short stories with song lyrics at the end of each chapter, mainly about life after Hollow. Although the book is put together in chapter format, they are not necessarily in sequential order in terms of an overall timeline of historical events. I wanted to feel less accountable for knowing (or not knowing) the specific times and dates of when the real events actually occurred, and there is a chance I have some of the details skewed according to my own perception, which is why I wrote this book in this particular format (a memoir). Instead, I will share my experience and my reactions without the pressure of having to cross-check all the exact facts in terms of times and dates, while still preserving the moral of the story, which has an optimistic ending. Keep in mind though, that the lyrics and the stories behind them are all based on actual events and I did my best to recount what actually happened. In other words, none of the stories are made up just for the sake of writing a song.

Read on with care and beware that I am about to tell you the story of how a man shot my mother and got away with it, leaving me with feelings of rage, pain, regret, anxiety, revenge, and ulti-mately a deep sense of loss of something that will likely never be recovered. You too might feel emotional when reading this.

One final, more positive note: I have made great progress in terms of healing from this tragic event, which, believe me, I never thought was possible. My life was a dark wreck at one point, and I saw some very low times. I was convinced that I was predeter-mined to be plagued by misery, anger, and despair. I thought I was destined to a life where anxiety for me and my family was the norm. I was wrong. My intent is not to put out a sob story of how bad I had it, nor to throw anyone under the bus, so to speak. On the contrary, I hope to show the reader that they are not alone in their life's story. Many of us have lived with trauma for far too long and we must realize the impact it has on people around us. Imagine what you could do with your life if you were free from the pain of your past and your self-limiting beliefs! I hope this book motivates you to get up and face the inner fear and challenge your doubts. Let's heal and move on together.

~Jake

* * *

Publisher's Note

This publication is written to provide the reader with authoritative information in regard to the subject matter covered. It is sold with the understanding that the publisher is not engaged with providing any legal, psychological, medical, financial, or other professional services or advice. This book is the author's account of experiencing trauma and the lasting impact it has had on his life, in addition to how he engages in a healing process using music as a coping mechanism. If expert and/or professional counseling is needed, the services of a professional should be sought.

Part 1: Melodies from Memories

"One good thing about music,
when it hits you,
you feel no pain."

Bob Marley

1

The Phone Call

It was a Tuesday morning in May. The sun was beginning to shine in through the bedroom window and the temperature outside seemed comfortable. Like every other morning before school, my siblings and I woke up to an alarm, turned on the morning radio show to get us up and out of bed, and then slowly started moving, looking for any extra motivation to go to school. We lived in an old, white, beat up farmhouse on a decent amount of property - about 40 acres of woods, and even though it was only rented, we didn't know the difference or even care whether my dad actually owned it or not. It provided a home for us that we could call our own for once and we learned a lot about hunting and fishing while we lived there.

My brothers and I shared a bedroom on one end of the up-stairs hallway, while my older sister and half-sister were at the other end in their own room. The rooms were separated by a bathroom in between, but close enough to hear one another's radio. On this particular morning, my sister was listening to one of her favorite morning shows, when we heard the following broadcast:

"Breaking news this morning from the Muskego Police Department—over the weekend there were multiple gunshots reported, and a young woman was found dead in her parent's living room. Another man was found with a gunshot wound to his stomach and is in critical condition. No names have been released yet. More details to follow as we get them in… now back to Bob and Brian in the morning."

The thought hit my sister first: *Mom lives in Muskego… Could it be? Nah, couldn't be.* I was in third grade and didn't pay attention too closely; I had breakfast on my mind. My oldest brother was in the bathroom getting ready for school. I finished getting dressed and went downstairs to pour a bowl of cereal.

Down in the dining room, my dad was drinking his coffee, getting ready for grandpa's morning phone call. His dad (my grandpa) would call every morning at 8:00 a.m. Although Dad acted like it was a chore to listen to Grandpa talk about life's most mundane events in long, drawn-out detail, in reality I could tell deep down he enjoyed it, or at very least gained some sort of purpose or duty out of it. I sat alongside him most days and could listen in on the conversation. My dad would make hand gestures to me pretending his hand was Grandpa's mouth as he turned his fingers into a puppet. We would laugh on the side as Dad would roll his eyes at me, indicating that Grandpa was yapping away, talking about the weather, his breakfast, when he last took out the garbage, and things of that simple nature.

On a side note, Grandpa played a key role in my story of recovery. Just to quickly foreshadow, I ended up living with him after a major turning point in my young life, and if it weren't for his stability, I cannot really even imagine how things would have ended up. He was a simple man but also a role model for us. We often called him "the machine," because he seemed to carry on with life as if he could somehow take the emotion out of any problem and work through it. He would keep us grounded and regulated and often shared stories about his hardships and struggles, especially growing up on a farm. He had to do his chores *before* walking to school, and a day off for him was practically unheard of. He looked forward to going to school, which not only provided him a break from the farm life, but ultimately empowered him to get out of the farm-life-cycle. He left his family's farm when he was just 18, joined the army, and eventually moved to the city, which is where we (my siblings and I) spent most of our later childhood years living, in his house.

Back to the story though and how Grandpa would call my dad every morning to check in. I was about two bites into my cereal when the phone rang as expected. The conversation that followed, however, was not at all about Grandpa's morning routine. This was a moment that changed our lives forever.

"Good morning," Dad said as he picked up the phone. "Sit down? What do you mean sit down?" he asked with a sense of urgency. "Just tell me. I can take it. Damn it, tell me what's going on!" My dad was sounding impatient and also frantic, and I could tell something bad had happened. "God damn it, Dad, just tell me what happened!" Now he was finally sitting, and I could tell that Grandpa had news for him that he would not share until his fatherly instincts were satisfied that my dad was sitting down. I dropped my spoon in my cereal bowl and couldn't move. "Oh no," he replied, with one hand on his forehead and the other grasping the phone. "She's dead? Are they sure? What the hell happened?"

I immediately panicked and ran upstairs to find my siblings. "Guys! Come quick! Someone died! I think it might be grandma!" My brother and sister and I huddled in our bedroom for what seemed like an eternity, our minds racing to try to make meaning out of the terrifying conversation I had just heard and tried to share with my older companions. We leaned over the railing to try to listen in.

"I'll have to go tell the kids," we heard as Dad hung up the phone and made his way upstairs. He got to the top and walked into our bedroom. Arms stretched out, he pulled us in and squeezed us like we have never been squeezed before. "I'm so sorry, kids. I'm so sorry." He couldn't find the words immediately, but the grip of his hug already told a far greater story than he could find the words for. "Your mom is gone. She died last night."

2

Hollow

The old farmhouse we lived in at the time gave us access to a twenty-two-acre lake and forty-four acres of woods, trails, and fields. On an average day, we spent most of our free time fishing, swimming, hiking around, hunting, or simply exploring life in the woods. Since Mom and Dad's divorce a few years prior, Dad always seemed to find a farm-style house to rent for us. Although I felt embarrassed at the time by our old, beat-up house, now I am extremely grateful for those experiences. We discovered nature at these places, and when we were bored it didn't take long to go outside and find something fun to get into.

The downside is that Dad was seldom there. We had our moments of fun with him fishing and hunting, but the majority of my memories are of me wondering when and if he'd come back home. He was at the bar... a lot. Each of us kids had the three local bars' phone numbers memorized (8 O'Clock Pub was ***9568, Hunter's Nest ***1760, Romey's ***9913). The bartenders recognized our voices as well, and when we'd call they'd say, "Nope, Junior is not here, haven't seen him." The few times I went to work with my dad, who was a self-employed painter, we would end up spending half of the day in the bar instead of going to the job site. Every time the phone would ring, he and a handful of other patrons would yell out, "Tell them I'm not here!"

My siblings and I all got good at recognizing what Dad's car sounded like from a quarter mile away. That way, when he'd come home drunk from the bar, we could quickly pack up our stuff, turn off the TV, and run up to our rooms and pretend we were sleeping. Sometimes he would see the glowing TV screen, indicating it had just been turned off, and he'd come up to our bedrooms and talk to us. Those moments were often horrible. Sometimes the stories were sob stories about how hard he was working to raise us; other times they were mushy talks about how much he loved us. We were too young to know anything other than to pretend we were sleeping so that maybe he'd leave us alone and go to sleep. It never occurred to me how much he was hurting; I was too self-absorbed to think of anyone else, and I was too angry that my mom and dad were not there to be parents for me.

When the news of our mother's murder hit us, I don't know why, but I just went outside and began walking around the land near our old farmhouse. We all kind of wandered around on our own path, each of us choosing a different trail. I imagine I was in shock but also somehow instinctively knew to get up and walk. Walk. Cry. Breathe. Repeat.

One of my first feelings was a feeling of being totally ripped off. *Now I'll never get to live with Mom.* It seems like since our parents' divorce, our lives had gotten pretty tough. We didn't have a consistent home life, and when Dad couldn't pay the rent, we'd find ourselves living with Grandpa. Dad was strict in many good ways in that we had to keep our rooms clean, our clothes folded, and we all had chores to do on a daily basis. But on the other hand, Dad drank every day and would sometimes be gone until the bars closed or wouldn't come home at all. His rules didn't always make sense, and he'd sometimes wake us up when he got home and make us search for the TV remote or do something irrational like explain why he couldn't find something, and we just couldn't make any sense out of it. I recall staying up late, hoping he'd be home soon with dinner. We called all of the local bars to ask when he'd be coming home. Sometimes we'd hear someone in the background say, "Tell them we'll be home soon." Other times, he'd come home with a pizza from the bar.

We would fantasize that someday we'd live with Mom again. Maybe someday she'd come back and pick us up for good. In actuality, it would be more accurate to say that deep down I really just wanted Mom to come back home. The unpredictability of our home life from day to day was scary, and, as you can imagine, like all young children do, I wanted my mommy.

There was a semi-romantic backstory to the reason she was shot. Allegedly, she and my dad were *potentially* working on getting back together "for the kids' sake." This made her boyfriend (the alleged shooter) become very possessive and jealous. This all could be a glorified or glamorized coping mechanism though, I can't say for sure. It does, however, hold an important place in regard to how people process traumatic events; the stories we tell ourselves might be largely based on emotional and psychiatric survival. I'll leave that one up to the psychologists. Here is the story of how the events of that horrific night unfolded. I base this story off of what we were told by our older family members and the police report I acquired from the city where she lost her life, Muskego, Wisconsin.

***

It was my uncle's twenty-fifth birthday party. Many family members from my mom's side gathered at a local pub to celebrate, play volleyball, and enjoy some beers together. According to the bartender's report, my mom and her boyfriend were arguing off and on throughout the night, with the arguments getting more intense as the night progressed. He noted in the report that the boyfriend seemed aggressive and possessive toward her.

As the evening got cooler, my mom said she had to leave to go get some warmer clothes on. I later learned that the truth of the matter is that she didn't want to ruin her brother's birthday party by arguing with her boyfriend in front of everyone. She lived with her parents at the time, which was only a mile or so from the pub. The neighborhood where they lived was very close-knit in that everyone seemed to know everybody else. My mom had seven other siblings, and four of them lived in that same neighborhood in their own houses. So she left the party with her boyfriend and headed for home.

According to the police report, the neighbors directly across the street from my mom's (also grandparents') house overheard an argument between mom and her boyfriend as she got out of the car. "I just want my kids back!" is what they heard her yelling toward him as she ran in the house. He followed. Gunshots rang out soon thereafter. The police report stated that his car was running in the driveway when they got there and his glove box was left open.

The adults at the bar were concerned that Chris (my mom) was taking longer than expected to come back. Two of my cousins, who lived up the street, were called to go check on her. What they said next changed their—and all of our— lives forever. I can't imagine what my cousins went through as they were the first ones on the scene; and they were just young teens.

"Uncle, help, come quick! Aunt Chris is lying on the floor! There's blood everywhere! Help!" My cousin's voice over the phone was filled with terror. My uncle could have probably run there faster than driving his car; this was his sister we're talking about. Plus, he was an athletic young man in his physical prime. He and his fiancée (now my aunt) jumped in their car and raced to their parents' house to see what was going on. On their way to the house, they passed a police car and started flashing their head-lights at it, indicating that they needed the cop to follow them. Not to mention, they were driving at a crazy speed to get there as fast as humanly possible, so this triggered the police officer to begin pursuit. Ironically, the cop held up about a quarter mile from the house and instead parked his car sideways in the middle of the road, perhaps responding to orders he received over his radio. At any rate, Uncle Scott had to go in alone.

When he arrived on the scene he found his sister lying lifeless on the living room floor, her sweater soaked in blood. Her boy-friend was moaning as he lay upright against the wall holding the gun in one hand and clutching his stomach in the other. Panic and rage set in. My uncle picked the TV up off of the stand and threw it at the guy. He grabbed the gun, not sure whether to shoot the man or let the police sort it out. The neighbors reported that my uncle's fiancée was yelling something like, "Don't shoot him!" He aimed the gun at him anyhow, and at the last second turned his aim at the wall next to him and fired the remaining bullets out of the gun's chamber.*

When the police and detective arrived, they reported that Chris Ellen Paul was dead and that her alleged shooter, Bill L., was in critical condition with a gunshot wound to his stomach. The police report states that the detective rode along with Bill in the ambulance to the hospital to try to get information from him. They said that he was mumbling, "Why did you shoot me, Chris?" The interesting thing is that the gun was registered under Bill's name, his car was left running in the driveway, the glove box and gun case were also left open in his car, and there was gunpowder residue on his hands. According to the forensic report, my mom had gunpowder on her sweater and bullet fragments, indicating that her wound was reported to be from point blank—meaning the gun was pressed up against her chest prior to being fired. The story I heard is that Bill then turned the gun on himself and shot himself in the stomach, later reporting that she shot him first and that he shot her back in self-defense. The detectives stated it was clear that foul play had ensued as things were broken and knocked off of the tables, but it was difficult for them to determine who was shot first. Due to the nature of the crime scene, and without a confession, Bill would not be charged or prosecuted.

The floor has dropped out, the rug has been pulled out from under our feet, my insides are numb, part of me is gone forever, I am hollow.

*I am forever grateful for my uncle and will never fully comprehend what he had to go through. The love I feel inside cannot be put into words. There is much more to this story that I learned later as an adult after speaking directly to him, which I am choosing to leave out of this book.

"HOLLOW"
©Jake Paul (ASCAP)
He put his car in park
left the engine runnin
opened up his glove box
pulled out his gun
and then he put it to her chest
sent his hollow point flyin
left her on the concrete floor to die.

When the news came across on the telephone line
I was went walking down my path alone, cryin
coping with the life I own when I decided
that never will I ever give up
Keep Tryin!

And those who speak the most
Never have much to say
Got a big black hole
In my restless soul
With no place to stay

He left me black like a crow
Colder than the snow
I think about her every day
By the way,
I'm hollow today

Now I can't help when you do good
you go get praised that way
you get mad when I do bad
but I was raised that way

These roots run deep
I can't sleep
I can't eat
I can't even breath
Can't hide from these images inside no more
I won't run from the one with the gun no more

And those who speak the most
Never have much to say
Got a big black hole
In my restless soul
With no place to stay

He left me black like a crow
Colder than the snow
I think about her every day
By the way,
I'm hollow today

So don't forget to say goodbye
you're never too young to die
Remember just to say goodbye
you're never too young to die

3

Providence

PROV·I·DENCE; NOUN - THE PROTECTIVE CARE OF GOD OR OF NATURE AS A SPIRITUAL POWER.

Throughout my childhood I recall my dad saying from time to time, "Everything happens for a reason." Those words were reassuring during the most difficult times of our lives; they provided a possible rationale to explain the bad things that happened to us. This way of explaining life, especially when we were struggling through something, gave me a sense that there was a Guardian Angel looking over me and that God had a plan for me.

About two weeks prior to our mom's death, my brother, sister, and I were spending time at our Aunt Lynne's house, one of my mom's older sisters, who also lived in the neighborhood. I was playing basketball outside when Aunt Lynne came out and said, "Hey, kids, your mom is on the phone, and she wants to take you out to dinner within the next few days. Where do you want to go?"

As I said earlier, my parents had divorced a few years before, and my dad had primary custody over us, so we lived with him. That meant that we would sometimes visit Mom on the weekends, but we stayed with Dad the majority of time. To be honest, we didn't see our mother very often. Over the years, our moments spent with her were getting few and far between. She hung out with a group of Harley-Davidson Riders, aka bikers. Now that I look back at those memories, I kind of assume they were like her other family.

Since we hadn't seen our mother for what seemed like months, my brother and sister and I were kind of shocked that she had called to take us out somewhere. We wondered why Mom, out of the blue, would call and ask us where we wanted to go to dinner. Was there some sort of occasion we were unaware of? We were so excited that our minds went blank. "Uh... how about McDonald's?" we asked. My aunt laughed as she put her mouth back to the phone and said, "Boy, Chris, your kids are a cheap date."

A few days later, Mom did come to pick us up, and we decided on *Chuck E. Cheese* (pizza) instead. She brought her boyfriend, Bill, with her, which was a new and even more awkward experience for us all. The first thing that struck me was that this guy seemed pretty old. I know now that he was in his early fifties, while my mom was only in her early thirties. She had married my dad when she was only eighteen and had my older sister shortly thereafter. By the time she was in her early twenties, she had already been married, divorced, and became a mother of three young children. I can certainly try to understand the pressure she must have felt as a young parent with life coming at her a little too fast, but I could never see why she was dating this old man she brought with her to our family outing. It just didn't seem right.

My next memory of Bill was of me sharing my chips with him. Actually, my intention wasn't to share. I opened my chips, and he grabbed one. I was naturally shy already, but this guy was cringy. There wasn't much about him that seemed friendly or warm towards kids. When I look back at the police report and think about *his* gun, *his* jealousy, and *his* possessiveness, I wonder how he could have gone through the actions he went through that awful night, knowing that there were three little kids who'd be left without a mother.

Above all of my own judgments about the way things played out, there was in fact a higher purpose directing it all. *Providence* is about the only word that fits my understanding of it all, because, in hindsight, I find it totally mind boggling that she called us so close to her death. I mean, what would spark her motivation to reach out to us kids then, when we hadn't heard from her for such a long time? Did she sense that the end was near? Why would she bring *him* with her? Was it a totally random chance that we got to meet him and see her two weeks before that horrific night? I choose to believe otherwise; there must have been a higher reason.

Don, The Guardian Angel

Life as a child for me was full of action, some of it was productive, most of it was just flat out dangerous. The older I got, the more risky the behaviors were, whether it involved me doing jumps over people on my BMX bike, racing motocross style dirtbikes through fields, boxing the neighborhood kids, or jeopardizing my overall health (and the well-being of the people around me at the time). The law eventually caught up to me and I was unable to get a driver's license when I turned 16 due to all the trouble I had already gotten into. My at-risk behaviors didn't slow down quite yet and fast forward a few more years and I was coming back home from college as a result of failing all of my classes.

Luckily for me, one thing I always had throughout all of this turmoil was ambition. I knew I had to work so I got a job at a machine shop and rode my bike 9 miles there and 9 miles home after my shift was completed at 11pm. That machine shop in Cudahy is where I met my first Guardian Angel, Don.

Don Joers was a white haired, pointy nosed, bib-overall wearing machinist. Imagine a much thinner version of Santa Claus and you'll have a pretty close idea of what he looked like. He even wore the thin framed glasses that he would slide up or down his long pointy nose when reading something to me. He introduced me to biblical passages and quotes and often times he would handwrite something from the Bible onto a note card and give it to me when I got to work. He had cassette tapes as well of him speaking at his church and explaining spiritual messages, and I would listen to them on the community bus or on my bike ride home. He had a very warm presence about him and to see him laugh and not laugh alongside him was nearly impossible, it was contagious and about as pure as watching a baby laugh. I later learned that he was a missionary and traveled to the country of Tobacco often with his wife and I was lucky enough to meet her once at their home in Sussex, WI. He invited me over for a dinner party and I was impressed by the natural beauty of the things in his life; his wife, their nice clean home, and all of their flower gardens all seemed like they required very little effort on his part. We spent a half hour just going through a tour of his yard and gardens, which was not something I expected from an old machinist. He praised God for all of it.

I'm not going to focus on God or religion here, but I do have to say that he instilled some HOPE within me. And when I started believing in something more, something more began to happen. The problem was that I didn't believe in anything other than that my life had been plagued by bad circumstances. I thought life was a lonely, unfair deal with lonely, unfair people, and I certainly didn't see any hope in sight.

Don Joers claimed that God had sent him to me. Based on the miracles I've experienced since meeting Don, I now have to agree.

The weird thing to me now is that I never saw any of that trouble as a hindrance or as something that defined me as a person. I knew inside that I had a purpose. To put it another way, I always knew deep down inside that I was going to come out on top; it was like this was some sort of training, or perhaps purging, that I had to go through. Don reminded me that *He chastises those He loves*, and that always rang through my head in times when I got myself in deep trouble.

Don gave me a student Bible that explained each reading and also included additional, real life stories to supplement each chapter. I remember the purple and black cover of this book very vividly, and I also remember that it had over 1,100 pages. I worked with Don at a machine shop in the city of Cudahy, and when I was ready to go back to college, I took it with me, which is where I experienced the most profound miracle of my entire life thus far.

The Miracle of Ezekiel, "TURN & LIVE"

On a very windy Friday night at the university, I was walking around in the middle of campus by myself. I knew I had to make big changes in my life, so I was trying to avoid the party scene and the people I typically hung around with. I was torn because although I enjoyed the company of my college friends at that time, I was also terrified inside about the things I would do when I was out at parties with them. I felt like I had a Jekyll and Hyde personality. On the one hand I was a shy, polite, and ambitious student who enjoyed getting up earlier than the average person and hitting the gym. On the other hand, I was a raging animal with an insatiable thirst for the nightlife action with all the thrills and excitement that came with it. The energy I felt deep inside when it was time to *just get ready* to party seemed to be a little out of proportion than everyone else, if you know what I mean. (By the way, if you don't know what I mean, I'm jealous of you!)

So on this particular night I grabbed my Student Bible and wandered around campus to look for a spot out of the wind to do some reading and reflecting. I thought it would be kind of cool too to be in the midst of this wind storm while reading my Bible. Besides, I was experiencing an emotional storm of my own. I was troubled by my dad's lack of involvement with his kids, and I was super upset about his heavy drinking; I didn't want to end up like him. In his own words, *he didn't want me to be like him either.* The challenge though, is that I was beginning to believe that perhaps I was destined to follow in his footsteps.

This is where things get interesting...

It was dark, I was walking under a streetlight, and it got incredibly windy. Either I accidentally dropped the book somehow or it flew out of my hands and landed on the ground—doesn't really matter at this point. The pages started blowing like crazy and I recall hearing the sharp, crispy, crackly sound of the paper rapidly blowing from page to page. Then suddenly it stopped. I bent down to pick up the book and saw that it had landed on a page called "Destined to Drunkenness?" (page 808-809). The format of this Student Bible is essentially a biblical passage followed by an extra blurb or explanation of the passage. In this case, it was Ezekiel 18: 1-20 where The Lord explains that regardless of what has happened we all have the ability and responsibility to *turn and live!* The blurb or extra explanation that went with it was about a boy who was afraid of being set up by a dead-end fate that he had no control over. God reminded him that he was born with free will and always had a choice in the matter.

> "NO WAY! HOW IS THIS POSSIBLE!?!?" I thought to myself. I read it again and again and realized that God had sent me this message loud and clear. It was time to take responsibility for not only my actions, but also what I believe. I believe in miracles.

This experience left a profound impact on the way I saw my life and the events that occured in it. Once again, I was a believer and a witness to something very powerful of which I had no logical explanation for. I knew then and I know now that a Higher Power is watching over us.

* * *

I had a friend who was also struggling with addictions in his life, so I gave that Bible to him. But I recently felt compelled (twenty-five years later) to get my hands on another copy of the same version of the book to try to recall and validate my experience. I started to have doubts about whether that page really existed in that version of the student Bible I had. As the doubt crept in, I started to wonder if I dreamt up that whole thing and the experience of the Bible blowing open to that specific page was an embellishment, exaggeration, or possibly a figment of my imagination. So I ordered another copy through Amazon and it arrived a few days later, on a Sunday of all days. I opened it and found the exact page and passage. I am still amazed that this even happened. Coincidentally, my old friend, who I gave my original copy to, messaged me on social media that same night to *razz* me about my favorite football team, the Green Bay Packers. I hadn't heard from him in many, many years. I always wondered what had motivated him to suddenly and randomly contact me then?

One major way that I changed the trajectory of my life is that I changed my outlook on the things that happened; I now see that there are no such things as meaningless coincidences. When I felt compelled to form a band and create music, I found each band member in similar fashion, where the circumstances that lead up to us meeting one another are beyond basic coincidence. How do I know? Because of the energy that was pulsating through my veins when I met each one of them. These experiences are what I call acts of Providence and now that I look back, I've had experiences like this my entire life. That is why I titled my third album The Providence EP.

Album Cover for Jake Paul Band's 3rd Album, "The Providence EP." Band Members: Jake Paul (vocal/guitar), John Gimler (keys), Chad Layton (vocal/lead guitar), Dan Zarwell (bass), Mike Balestreri (drums/vocal) Recorded & Engineered at Cherry Pit Studios 1. Indestructible 2. Road Trip 3. Balance 4. Inhale
@danzarwellphotography

4

Don't Forget

"WHEN MY TIME IS UP I HOPE IT'S WELL UNDERSTOOD, AND DON'T FORGET, I DID THE BEST THAT I COULD."

It is safe to say my mom and dad's relationship was definitely in turmoil long before they split up. Thinking back, both of my parents were extreme in many ways, and it seemed as though neither of them would back down to anyone, including each other.

Dad would often come home late with various injuries from fights he'd gotten into at the bar. He'd gotten his two front teeth punched out once, been thrown to the gravel on a few occasions, and we even found him sleeping in grandpa's bathtub one morning. He explained that his bloody tongue was from being kicked in the mouth by someone who knew Tae Kwon Do. Although he claimed that he ended up victorious at the end of these brawls, they certainly came with physical injuries to him and emotional wounds to us kids.

Living with the fear of not knowing if, or when, a parent is coming home safe is also traumatic. To examine this a bit closer, it's like this: part of the trauma is in the actual events of what we saw happen, another part comes from what we think *might* happen next, and yet there is a whole new level of trauma in regard to having to process and attempt to make sense out of what was becoming our new *normal.* And by the way, none of it was predictable, stable, or made any sense to me. In other words, my concept of what normal is, was a confusing web of inconsistent and unpredictable, irrational, often violent, and terrifying behaviors. I was getting used to and accustomed to feeling anxious because something at any moment was bound to happen.

One *normal* evening when Mom was still alive, she came to visit us at my grandpa's house (the same grandpa who made the phone call). Grandpa's house was a basic, single-story, one-bathroom, three-bedroom, ranch style house. It had a cozy yet small kitchen, so if you were sitting on one side of the kitchen table you could see into the living room, but if you were on the other side of the table you could see out the kitchen window into the driveway. I recall sitting on my mom's lap while she was playing cards at the kitchen table. We were sitting on the side that could see out into the driveway. It was a warm summer night, and the windows were open to allow the breeze to come in. Life was good for a brief moment.

Suddenly I heard a rumbling sound coming up the street. It sounded scary to me, and it was getting louder and closer. It seemed to turn from a subtle rumble to a loud, angry roar. It was the sound from a group of Harley-Davidson motorcycles.

Mom was what you would call a "biker chick." As far as I can remember she was hanging out with Harley riders. After my parents' divorce, my dad would take us to bars and to church festivals with him. On one occasion, we coincidentally bumped into mom, who was with her biker friends. She was wearing a black leather vest and a blue do-rag bandana on her head. She knelt down to get eye level with me and handed me a five-dollar bill to play games with. Then she was off again, like a phantom, in and out of our lives at unpredictable moments.

Back to the story of sitting with mom and grandpa at the kitchen table. The loud rumbling sound was coming from two or three bikers who pulled into the driveway. I heard my mom say that it was Dave, who was her boyfriend at the time. Although I was too young to understand how relationships worked, I later understood that Dave must have been Mom's first boyfriend after her and Dad divorced. I had seen him before at her home in Milwaukee, but I really didn't know much about him, other than he often breathed heavily, was slightly overweight, and had a skinny, long-haired side kick who went by the name "Snake."

On this particular night, Dave brought his friends with him, and I'm assuming they were not happy to find my mom at my dad's house. When my mom looked out the window and realized who was there, she immediately tried to put me down and push me under the table. Dad came charging into the kitchen from the living room area and said, "Watch out, I'm going downstairs to grab my gun." Dad's room was in grandpa's basement, and in order to get to the stairs to his bedroom, he had to pass through the kitchen.

Seconds later he came running up with his .30-.30 rifle. The next thing I knew, there were shots fired in grandpa's driveway. Then I heard the motorcycles start up and the bikers were gone.

Apparently my dad shot at the ground beneath their bikes to scare them off. I have no idea what was said prior to this or after this, but I do know that sirens were all over grandpa's driveway soon thereafter. We watched out the window while dad was handcuffed and put into a squad car and taken away.

***

That experience evolved into the first verse of a song I titled **"Don't Forget."** It is about the underlying story beneath our dad's messages that, *Even though you may think I came up short, don't forget that I did my best.* He had kind of a Rocky Balboa side to his personality, which would inspire him to say great and wonderful things, but he also went through some very depressing life circumstances regarding some close friends who died young (several from suicide), and that ultimately shaped his outlook on life. His attitude became one of, "None of us will make it out of here alive," (verse 3) and he seemed to carry an undertone in a *why even bother trying* sort of attitude.

My dad's shortcomings bothered me deeply, which caused me intense anger. I wanted him to be there for me. He wasn't at my sporting events, my award ceremonies, my parent-teacher conferences, and he most certainly never took me to the doctor when I was injured or ill. The majority of my memories of him were of him being drunk. So this song was my way of distorting my perception of the whole situation to make it less dire… maybe for the sake of emotional survival. I needed to reframe the situation before it completely turned me toxic. I flipped the self-pity that flooded my being as the result of having an alcoholic absentee father into a hero figure who did what he had to do based on the circumstances that life threw at him. And for all I know, maybe that is exactly how things are supposed to play out.

In the end, I believe he did do the best he could with what he knew. So I cut him loose, in a metaphorical way, and forgave him for not living up to my expectations. The events in the song are in fact true, but the messages about hope, ambitions, dreams, and so on are a fantasy about what I wish he would have said to me.

The good news is that I get the opportunity to say those words to my own kids when they need me in their own times of trouble. And to set the record straight, I believe alcoholism is in fact a disease from which my dad suffers, and I am not faulting anyone with a disease. He in fact did do the best that he could, and I love him for what he instilled in us as a father in our early years.

"Don't Forget"

©Jake Paul (ASCAP)

Once daddy told me

when I was young

step aside boy

I'm going down stairs

to grab my gun

And when he came back

with it loaded with one

he was so raw

made the outlaws run

(next page)

He shot at the ground

beneath their feet

they took off real quick

right down that street

they never did come back

to admit defeat

The cops came with cuffs

and threw dad in the

backseat

Once dad told me

before I grew up

you better at least try

don't be afraid to screw up

and when you get down

I know just what to do

put your arms around my waist

and squeeze 'til I turn blue

(pre chorus)

Dad told me

when I was a young teen

you gotta have hope, ambitions, and dreams

'cuz life doesn't always go the way

that it seems

so I pray that you make it

through the valleys and the streams

(chorus)

And when my time is up

I hope it's well understood

don't forget

I did the best that I could

when my days are over

I hope you understand

my man

and don't forget

I did the best that I can

Daddy showed me

when I was young

how to be a man

and stand up to anyone

but when we got home

we were all stunned

to see him sleeping in the bathtub

with a bloody tongue

Dad showed me

how to deal with girls

when they play their mind games

try to mess with your world

Don't ever take their fits man

but give'em a whirl

make'em feel like they're better

than a diamond or a pearl

(bridge)

He said I want you to be a star

I never really did get far

I'm stuck here at the bar

I see the sunshine

On your life, not mine

And everything is gonna work itself out just fine

(pre chorus)

(then chorus)

And when my time is up

I hope it's well understood

don't forget

I did the best that i could

when my days are over

I hope you understand

my man

and don't forget

I did the best that I can

Daddy taught me

when I was young

how to keep my cool

no matter what

havin' all this fun

The secret that he knows

that helps him survive

is none of us will make it

out of here alive

Dad told me

when I was a young man

you gotta have fun

anyway that you can

cuz life doesn't always go

the way that you planned

you don't gotta be the best

be the best that you can

And when my time is up

I hope it's well understood

don't forget

I did the best that I could

"When my days are over

I hope you understand my man

and don't forget

I did the best that I can."

5

Keep Your Demons

"AM I AN EVIL MAN WITH A HOLY SPIRIT

OR AN EVIL SPIRIT IN A HOLY MAN?"

Not to overstate the obvious, but our lives were tumultuous and often unpredictable. The amount of emotional extremes on the regular was just too much to process in my mind. These intense events were becoming not only my family's norm, they were also defining me into an identity or persona in regard to who I was deep down as a person. I (or something) was crafting a story in my head, and the self-talk was that I was bad and had to be on the lookout for threats, which meant I always had to prove how bad I was. My alter ego had been born.

Further, the the idea that my mom died from a gunshot wound to her chest and her assailant is still on the loose had destroyed any sense of "goodness" left inside. I was in complete shock and really didn't talk to an adult about it or process the emotions that come with circumstances like that. It was like I had a hot coal inside my chest and didn't know how to cool it off. We just "dealt" with it on our own, which created great turmoil within my family. We had been suddenly traumatized and shell-shocked, the rug had been pulled out from under our feet, and nothing made sense anymore.

My dad's way of dealing with life was that he was gone a lot. He'd be out at the bars daily and nightly, basically leaving us kids to fend for ourselves. I don't recall ever being able to go to a snack cupboard or open the fridge and find any food. Obviously we ate, and our situation was not entirely void of any nourishment, but what I'm saying is my perception had totally changed by then into a distortion of extremes. "We were so poor, so different, so disadvantaged, so unlike anyone else" is the message I carried around with me. When I would hear about other people's misfortunes, my mind would quickly start building a case inside and start saying "well that is not as bad as my situation."

My oldest sister became our primary caretaker, making us some of our favorite snacks like "sugar toast" or "saltines and sugar-butter." She worked at a local restaurant and would give us some money from time to time to buy snacks from the grocery store—what a treat! I do recall random people dropping off boxes of food at our house for us, and it was during that time of our lives that social services got involved to investigate if we were being neglected. Spoiler alert: we were.

My older brother and I dealt with life in our own unique ways, but one thing we had in common in terms of how we coped was that we both got into a lot of trouble in and out of school. Overall, I was a good student-athlete when I tried to be. But the appeal to be someone regarded as "bad" was something that took priority over getting good grades. I somehow felt powerful by being bad. Therefore, I had to be the *baddest*.

My younger brother was placed into foster care because he had a different mother than me and his mother was caught up in all sorts of bad behaviors. She moved to Arizona and took him with her and my dad couldn't get custody of him. Her drug addiction got her put into jail and that meant my little brother was placed into foster care - we hadn't seen or heard from him for over a year after that.

I was in third grade when my mom passed. Ironically, that is when I got into my first fight at school. Maybe I was mad at the injustice of my world and couldn't take any misdoings from other people anymore? Who knows, but now that I am a teacher, I find it troublesome to see young children get into physical fights. For this particular fight I got into, a boy was not playing kickball fairly and he took the ball away from another kid and started causing all sorts of stress in our game. I stepped in to set him straight and the next thing I knew we were punching each other in the face. I came out of it with a chipped tooth, looking and feeling like "a chip off the ol'block." I was involved in several other fights throughout my time in school, and they all seemed to stem from me not liking someone who was treating someone else badly.

In hindsight, that is also when I started making my first songs. I was writing and attempting to record music on a cassette player way back in elementary school. I found myself writing lyrics during class a lot. I'd get a beat in my head and start adding words that helped describe how I felt inside or what was happening in my life at the time. I did this all throughout elementary, middle, high school, and college, and now have old notebooks full of lyrics. Music was, and still is, my escape.

In high school, sports became my outlet for anger and my salvation from boredom. I was lucky to have coaches that inspired me to work hard for them. I could tell they really cared about me, even though they knew my background and about all the trouble I was getting into. That made me want to gain their approval and acceptance. One of them even mysteriously "found" a new pair of shoes for me to run in. I broke a high school record for scoring the most touchdowns in a single football game, and I even made it to the state championship track meet in the long jump, despite being injured. I gave everything I had, because I wanted to make my coaches proud of me. The message here is that I was yearning for adult attention and approval and would go to any lengths to get it.

Despite my successes in sports, there were competing forces within me that would lead me into trouble. Eventually I found chemicals to do for me what I couldn't do for myself: feel safe. By the time I was fifteen, I was in enough trouble to have to see a drug and alcohol counselor. She "assessed" me as being chemically dependent. But, boy, did those chemicals make me feel a sense of exhilaration and freedom! There was no way I was giving them up. Unfortunately, those extreme reactions have an opposite and equal reaction. That is how the following song, "Keep Your Demons" came into being.

"Keep Your Demons"
©Jake Paul (ASCAP)

Waking up in a black & white world
with people knocking at my door
I gotta get up
gotta keep moving
there's too much to live for
I'm gonna climb the mountain
and get to the water
to wash my hands
Am i an evil man with a holy spirit
or just an evil spirit
in a holy man?

I can feel it creep down in my soul
Runnin' straight through my bones
You can keep your demons
I've got my own
I see the sunrise
through bloodshot eyes
And my heart feels like a stone
So you can keep your demons
I got my own

I was walking down this colorful road
people staring at me strange

I heard one of'em say
that I'm destined to stay
But I know that i'm gonna change
When I climb the mountain
and get to the water
to wash these hands
Am I an evil man with a holy spirit
Or just an evil spirit in a holy man, oh-man!

These demons demons demons
Just won't leave me alone
These demons demons demons
Just don't leave me alone
These demons demons demons
Just can't leave me alone
Leave me alone
Leave alone
I want to go home

Anamoly Records is the original
indie label all songs were registered
under (ASCAP).

6

In the End

"EVERYTHING THAT BEGINS MUST ALSO COME TO AN
END.
DON'T KNOW HOW, DON'T KNOW WHY, ONLY GOD KNOWS
WHEN."

Life after mom's death curved my behavior in ways that made me form an alter ego that often led me into serious trouble. I felt an elated, yet dangerous, sense of power with it all. I was suspended for fighting in school and to be honest, I didn't care much about anything. I certainly wasn't afraid of getting into trouble or facing consequences. I even started fantasizing about going to jail; at the time I thought it would be cool. Only later in life did I realize that it wasn't cool at all. It was a sad place for lost souls, and some people come out of it worse off than when they went in. I was determined to change my ways and my out-look on life.

If I was willing to consider the idea that perhaps we have a disease of the mind that tries to control our behavior in order to get what *it* wants, then perhaps I could let go of my anger towards life and the people in it and forgive the ones who I thought did me wrong. I mean, maybe, just maybe, this whole idea of being mad at our parents for not raising us right, or the idea of being mad at anyone for that matter for not living up to our expectations is kind of an overplayed drama. Could it be that all of this anger, sadness, anxiety, depression, rage, and despair was all the result of a big misunderstanding about how I *thought* people were supposed to be?

Perhaps all of the ideas about what I thought was supposed to happen in my life—you know, the normal family with two working parents who provided for their family while also nurturing and supporting their children's ambitions, goals, and dreams—was an illusion created by my own self-serving psyche. Let me rephrase something here: maybe just because things didn't work out the way I was under the impression they were supposed to, it doesn't mean I get to hold everyone responsible for not living up to my expectations. If everything does happen for a reason, then I've come to believe that the reason things happen is to help us become the best version of ourselves. I'm not trying to be super "holier than thou" here as if I'm just choosing to reframe everything - the fact is that my old way of seeing things and doing things wasn't working out so well.

When I broke those thoughts and questions down and worked through them in my own way, forgiveness and acceptance started to enter into my emotional state. The relief I had been yearning for started to enter my life without the use of chemicals. I finally began to see people as works-in-progress (including myself); they were all doing the best they could with what they knew and believed to be true. Love and acceptance came into my life, and for the first time in a long time I could actually look people in the eye and see them as a fellow participant in this drama of life. My perception shifted, and I realized that no one was doing things *to me*; I was no longer a victim of life's circumstances! I didn't have to judge others and carry my anger around any longer. Like a dam thats holding too much water, my walls built from anger were showing signs of cracking. The anxiety, fear, and anger were starting to release their hold on me.

* * *

In the end, I'm amazed at how everything worked out even though I couldn't see it at the time. In a metaphorical sense, I was wearing a dark pair of glasses made up of false beliefs that was inhibiting my ability to see clearly. There are a couple of key points that I learned and found useful in regard to acceptance, forgiveness, healing, and seeing things for what they are. I need to share them here; I know they will be helpful for you too if you apply them to your view of other people.

- Behavior is a symptom - what is the driving force behind their action?
- Behavior is a form of communication - what are they trying to communicate by acting like that?
- Being a victim gave me a sense of purpose; unfortunately it also fed into the negative cycle I was trying to break
- Forgiveness is an emotional state of healthy being that may need daily maintenance

- Practically every generation blames their parents for the way they were raised if things don't work out the way they had hoped it would

> Every story has happy moments and sad moments. It ain't over until you decide it's over. If you are experiencing a sad ending to your story, then maybe it's time to stop reading it and start writing it.

"In the End"
©Jake Paul (ASCAP)

Nobody ever knew

what you were going through

after all of these years

even I never knew

I'm so sorry that I judged

it was so easy to blame

my troubles on the one

who raised me up, gave me my name

I can finally see

a life full of joy

you were my hero man

when I was a boy

so let's move on

together again

Everything is

gonna work itself out

In the end

Everything that begins

must also come to an end

I don't know how

don't know why

only God knows when

Every enemy

that I've ever had

was my friend

kinda funny how it works out

In the end

When I heard the news

that we got this disease

I said I will not lose

and I refuse to freeze

But I'm fresh out of money

and I ain't got no time

give me the shovel

I'll find the answer to this puzzle

buried deep in my mind

Now that I got this thing solved

it's clear

I resolve to live my life

without fear

and I can smile to myself

with a beautiful grin

at how everything works out

In the end

Everything that begins

must also come to an end

I don't know how

don't know why

only God knows when

Every enemy

that I've ever had

was my friend

kinda funny how it works out

In the end

So can you understand

what I been going through?

you're just a sheep like me

and I'm a slave like you

> and everything that I've achieved
>
> is my attempt to cope
>
> on an ocean of emotion inside
>
> just trying to stay afloat

So let's move on, together again

man I know what you're about

don't you break, just bend

everything is gonna work itself out in the end

it's time for you and I

to go out and have fun again

| 62 |

7

Move On

I experienced a blissful sense of freedom when I decided to write this book about my songs and where they came from. By giving them away to you, so to speak, they live on and I can move on. That is the deal, don't get stuck in one place. If you are stuck, there is blockage holding you there. By blockage I mean thought patterns, beliefs, fears, or misunderstandings. I'd say you owe it to yourself to take action, even if it is just a small step.

Even though I was once angry and hopeless, life is now one thousand times better for me. This new view is not a quick fix or a temporary mirage. I have so much gratitude and genuine joy for being able to experience life now, I feel like I don't have enough time to explore everything on my new wish list. I went from, "When is this going to be over, how much more of this can I possibly take?" to "I am lucky that I get to be a part of this. There is so much I am looking forward to."

If you are wondering how I legitimately changed, one thing I suggest is that you envision your dream often and continue to ask yourself, *What can I do today to make my life better?* I wrote that question in marker on a piece of paper and taped it to the back of my door in my bedroom at my grandpa's house when I was a young teen, and I had to read it every morning before I left the room in order to get the door open. I use the same mantra every morning as I get ready for the day.

By taking small steps every day, there will come a time when you arrive at a place in your life where you can let go of your past and truly move on, and you will see your life change before your very eyes. The weird thing to me is that my brain is telling me that everyone else around me has changed, I'm still me. I'm not kidding! If you are reading this and these words are striking a chord within you, I bet something is holding you back, something is blocking you, or something inside of you doesn't really want you to succeed. Your purpose is to discover it, uncover it, and discard what is not working any more.

The thing that was holding me back was my fear based alter ego. I feel like I was hijacked by it. It influenced my thoughts, my behavior, and my outlook on life. It talked me down a lot. It thrived off of my insecurities and wanted to keep me afraid and stuck in one old, dark, place, reliving the patterns I experienced from the trauma.

I do want to share that I experienced events directly as a child that were in fact traumatic and caused long-lasting effects for me, but I did not get into those specifics in this book. There are a few good reasons for omitting that information.

One, I want to share my story about the songs and how they were created as a result of, and coping mechanism for, my experiences. It's tough to word this properly, but I don't want to bring in other people's involvement too much in my own trauma recovery...mainly to protect everyone's integrity including my own.

Two, I used to listen to other people's stories and compare them to my own only to end up saying to myself, "my story is worse." Those words only held me back though, or kept me in the same mental, emotional, and spiritual place of self-pity and slowed down my own personal growth. If you've had trauma in your life, I know your trauma was very traumatic for you, and mine was for me. That's all there is to it.

Lastly, I didn't want this book to be categorized solely as a self-help book (although I do hope it helps anyone who reads it!). The bottom line is that yes, I had traumatic experiences in my life and I found a way to cope with those experiences in the form of music creation (more methods and strategies in Part 2). I also underwent a form of therapy called *EMDR.

When I see where my life is now I feel like shouting off the roof tops to those who are suffering and can't find a solution. I mean if you found a pot of gold would you keep it all to yourself or would you share it with anyone who looks like they could use a little gold in their life? I have found that gold, in a metaphorical sense, and it has little to do with picking apart other people's lives and the choices they felt they had to make. My recovery from trauma is about how I can be a better person today, and is not about airing out other people's dirty laundry or throwing them under the bus, so to speak.

If there is such a thing as identifying the most important step in my recovery I guess I'd have to say it is the realization that I am responsible for my life, the feelings in it, regardless of what happened to me. I took my power back by realizing that. In other words, I recovered it.

> "   What happened in the past is dead, I'm moving on   "
> instead.

*EMDR is a form of talk therapy called Eye Movement Desensitization Reprocessing. I was offered a free session while I attended college and took advantage of it because I was tired of waking up in the morning and feeling angry for no apparent reason (at least that I was aware of). The therapy was kind of like hypnosis, although I was awake and conscious during each session. I won't go into great detail here but I can summarize by saying that essentially I had memories locked away in my subconscious mind that I was unaware of. The therapy helped me bring those memories back into my conscious thoughts so that I could discuss and process them with a professional counselor. I am a fan of that therapy, although I believe it didn't "cure" me of anything. Rather, it gave a name to the root of my anger, which then helped me process it and move on.

HERE IS THE SIGN YOU'VE BEEN
LOOKING FOR!

"Move On"
©Jake Paul (ASCAP)

'Always knew there'd be a happy ending
just between me and you
I bet you never saw this one coming
I wonder if you'll see it through

They say everything that has a beginning
must also come to an end
I know nothing ever lasts forever
So why does everyone pretend?

I'm moving on instead
I'm moving on instead

There comes a time when we all realize
that everybody has their flaws
It's the one thing we all have in common
It's the one universal law

So forget what everybody said
I'm moving on instead
I'm moving on instead

What happened in the past is dead
I'm moving on instead

There's brighter days that lie ahead
I'm moving on instead

The future looks bright ahead
I'm moving on instead

The future looks bright ahead
I'm moving on instead

Part 2:

Harmony in Healing: The Tools That Mended My Soul

The stories and song lyrics in Part 1 describe what happened in my early life and how I used music and songwriting as a coping mechanism when I didn't know what else to do. The next section, Part 2, describes my path of deep self-reflection, post trauma, including the thought processes and philosophies that gave me the proper insights I needed in order to make the next move and take the next steps towards inner peace in my healing journey.

8

The Stigma of Being Traumatized

Extinguish the gaslight once and for all.

There is an unspoken stigma with admitting that I have been a victim of trauma and I can certainly understand why it took so long to admit it to anyone. Let's be honest, the vulnerability that is part of opening up about something that was traumatizing required a willingness to risk feeling the pain again. It is almost the same vulnerability that I experienced when I was initially traumatized. I mean, why would anyone want to subject themself to those feelings all over again? Not to mention, there is a conflict that occurs when people don't really understand one another. For example, not everyone understands the effects trauma has on someone's behavior nor can the experiencer understand what it may be like from the observer's point of view as well. There is a risky vulnerability needed to understand one another, and that applies to both sides of this equation.

I hope my story and experience gives you the needed support and inspiration to take the risk of being vulnerable again. Without acknowledging that you are an experiencer of trauma, you might as well say you are giving your power and your freedom to be happy and healthy away to the person or people who caused it to begin with. As someone who has gone through it, I'm telling you that you can (and should!) take it back. That is where the term "recover" comes from - you get to recover what was taken away from you.

I heard a trauma specialist explain once that it wasn't the event itself that actually caused the trauma, but the person's response to it. My response to it was a combination of anger, anxiety, restlessness, self-medicating, over-achievement, and many other extremes. It never occured to me though that all of my extreme behaviors were in response to being traumatized. I thought I was just trying to be *somebody.*

When I decided to actually sit down and commit to writing this book, I didn't take into consideration that I would have to relive many painful memories, not only from my perspective, but also through the perspective of all of the people who this book affects personally. After I processed those memories, I cried all over again and let the energy flow through me. It was cleansing.

You might wonder why I would want to *open that can of worms* or *dig up the past* like that but to be honest, it really wasn't a healthy option to *not* write this book. There is something larger than just me at play here; I believe I am breaking a cycle that has been hidden for many generations and although I am afraid at times, there is a deeper sense of meaning that is guiding me along the way.

I myself thought "Don't I now have the right to keep it buried and just live my life as I please? Can't I numb out the painful memories, brush them under the rug, and pretend to be normal like everyone else? I mean, everyone has a story about an imperfect family situation, can't I just live life and be blissful again like I was when I was a child?"

I wish. As a matter of fact, I tried that method for a long time and it just doesn't work.

Another thing that kept me in bondage of my past trauma was my inner dialogue about it:

"I already lived through it once, I'm not going through it again. I'm a grown adult, I can do what I want now and I don't have to ever go back there again."

And that is in fact my right too...as long as it is working for me and the ones I love. In my case, not acknowledging my past and trying to be normal like everyone else just wasn't working out. I wasn't feeling well (emotionally and physically) and had terrible anxiety most times, especially when interacting at social events. If I'm being honest, just the thought of interacting at social events would spike my anxiety.

When faced with the idea of sharing my story about trauma with the world, my inner dialogue went berserk, "Wait, I didn't ask to be traumatized when I was a kid. I trusted someone that I was instinctively drawn to trust and they hurt me...badly. And you expect me to bring that back to the surface of my life and share it outloud? For what reason? Don't you remember how mean people can be? Are you sure you aren't over-reacting to this whole situation? So and so had a rough go at it and you don't see them telling everyone about it. I mean, what will people think of you?"

And then on the other hand, by keeping it a secret inside I felt like I was doing something similarly harmful to my true self by spending so much energy maintaining the secret. It's no wonder I had anxiety!

I kept telling myself that *I am supposed to be stronger than this, less vulnerable than this, better than this, and I'm supposed to be able to deal with this as just a part of life. I am tough, I can do this.*

Eventually I got tired of trying to be something I am *supposed* to be. And where does this image or idea of who I'm supposed to be even come from anyway? Either way, I knew I was tired of living two lives and there came a moment when something inside me strongly "nudged"me to share my story of how I've been affected by childhood trauma. Thank goodness I took action.

* * *

Where does the gaslighting concept come from and how does it relate to trauma?

For those who don't know, gaslighting is a method used to gain control over someone through manipulation and by trying to break down the other person's trust in themself. In a general sense, it is when someone tries to convince another person that their feelings are wrong and they then try to get that person to second guess and doubt themself. It happens in abusive relationships where someone is harming another person, then says something to the effect of "Look what you are making me do to you? Why do you keep making me hurt you like this?"

One [unfortunate] fact of the matter is that when traumatic events do occur, not everyone has the capacity to be honest about it. That means that some people go into denial and will defend that denial without even realizing it. The urge to be right (instead of honest) can override logic and fact and that is a fact I had to accept. When I did accept that some people I know just cannot be honest with themself right now, I was then able to *extinguish the gaslight* and move forward with the healing process.

Who knows, maybe the gaslighters are not ready to acknowledge and feel the painful emotions that come with looking inward and being honest about what they see - I can feel compassion for those people without letting them manipulate my experience. I found that some people are genuinely supportive and proud that I spoke out, while some people deny it, almost or seemingly *trying* to make me feel guilty for saying anything to begin with. At any rate, I *did* experience trauma and had to do something positive about it or it would have destroyed my inner being - sharing my story turned out to bring a sense of release and relief that I didn't know I was missing out on. I can breath again! Did I mention my anxiety is now gone?

Not everybody is ready to heal and move on though. It does require being brutally honest with oneself and the capacity to feel some level of pain or discomfort. I liken it to the game "hot potato." Being honest with yourself might feel like holding onto a hot potato and the sooner you get rid of it, the better you feel. My take on the gaslighters is that they either can't stand the heat of being honest with themself or they have so many layers of denial covering up their own uncomfortable past that they don't even consider the idea of going back through their own past and healing any wounds within. It is just easier, or safer, or more comfortable for them to project outward (often onto people like you who are trying to do well for themselves).

I certainly can't fault anyone for not wanting to experience the discomfort (or pain) that is required to eventually find inner peace. That is why they say **it is not easy, but it is worth it.** What helped me in these situations is the realization that we are all hurt to some extent and we all are on a spectrum of healing. Being gaslighted lead me to realize that I had to strengthen my own personal boundaries, which once again, yielded a very high rate of return on my investment.

Let's turn it toward you for a moment. If you think that you are in fact strong enough and tough enough to handle your trau-matic past experience all by yourself, then be sure to get a 2nd and 3rd opinion on your perspective on how you are handling it. Your perception of yourself and how you are handling your affairs may not be in line with what the people who are closest to you think (wink, wink).

My experience can be paraphrased like this: I was under an assumption that maybe I was born angry, born with anxiety, born with an addictive personality, and ultimately born *broken*. I assumed things *are what they are* and I just need to learn how to accept that. I just need to do more or work harder...

Nothing could have been further from the truth.

In a general sense, I was lied to. I was told (or lead to believe) that I was a certain way because I was born that way. I was told that I had a really tough hand dealt to me and I was a victim of bad circumstances. Like Jim Carrey in the movie *The Truman Show*, I had a cast of characters in my social network that also supported my lifestyle that was built on values and beliefs that were not serving my own personal development very well.

Now I am not qualified to place the blame on who or what created that world view, but I am qualified to take responsibility for my own life. So I rejected the idea that I was born that way. I discovered that I was living a lie and the anxiety and anger were my signs and symptoms of living out that lie on a daily basis.

I knew in my heart that something was "off" about the way I was seeing the world and unfortunately (or fortunately I guess depending on how I reflect on it now) my social circles supported my victim mentality. Again, I am not placing blame here;

they didn't know any different either and I sure became the top salesman when it came to proving how unfortunate I was.

Ironically, now that I admitted that I experienced trauma as a kid and am taking action to heal from it, I am tougher, stronger, and more independent than I've ever been. I am not *hiding* the real me like I always had been in the past and I'm not living a double life anymore. I literally have zero anxiety in the sense that I used to have it where I would just wake up in the morning and feel a very unpleasant sense of doom. I now see and believe that the anxiety I carried around for years was my soul's way of telling me that it was time to stop spending so much energy trying to cover up a fake identity. The gaslight has been extinguished.

HERE I AM WORLD! READY OR NOT, HERE I COME!

9

Hello Acceptance. Goodbye Anxiety.

I didn't cause it. I didn't create it. So why was I trying so hard to control it?

Knowing what I now know about trauma and anxiety, I know that recovering from it and living a happy and peaceful life is totally possible. The challenge is that it is not only hard to see or imagine, many people don't want to look at "it" or themselves on that level of reflection (and perhaps they don't need to). It is uncomfortable. I think for most people, being upset, anxious, irritable, or angry at their life's circumstances allows them to stay put, so to speak. It feels safer to keep personal issues buried or hidden under our conscious awareness where nobody can see them. *Or so we think...

The reason this is such a hot topic for me is because now that I am on the other side of the change I always wanted to create, it is difficult to see others who want to do the same, but don't know how to. Like me, they are are too smart for their own good and have taken themself out of the game of possibility, so to speak.

They have not only created the rules by which they themselves cannot play by, they built the very trap by which they cannot escape from either.

Let me pause to clarify and qualify myself first - I escaped from the anxiety trap, but this is not about me gloating about how awesome my life is. If that is the vibe these words are putting out there, I am sorry for that. Trauma and anxiety are awful and can really screw people up. I'm trying to snap anyone who reads this out of a negative rut they might be stuck in - especially if you are like me where you were (or are) under the impression that life was (or is) just meant be be endured. You are missing something BIG here and I don't want you to wait until it's too late where you are ill, depressed, or missed out on being fully present on the things that really matter the most. Anxiety can take all of that joy and awareness away from you, but it doesn't have to be that way.

For real, on an average day, I am blessed with joy and gratitude and have been ever since I discovered something vital to my recovery: the anxiety was there to tell me something. How do I know this? Because I finally did what it was telling me to do (i.e. share my story and work towards healing) and now it is gone. **The anxiety I experienced for years is now gone.** It served its purpose and dissipated.

I was spending a lot of energy trying to convince myself that anxiety was a normal part of life in my family. "Maybe it is just a part of how I was made - that my life *is what it is*." The thought that I was supposed to simply accept life *as is* wasn't sitting right with me though. As a matter of fact, it was causing me deep inner despair and fear. I believed deep down inside that there must be a happier way to live. So why couldn't I find it?

I figured I must be doing something wrong and that I just need to work harder to figure out what it is. So I became very "busy."

Sitting still for me was tolerable for brief moments, but more less felt like wasting time. Why would I sit still when I could be working on something? *I'm burning daylight here people, get out of the way!* I started a business (get it, "busy-ness"), tried boxing, mixed martial arts, meditation, weight training, running, exercising, supplements, going to grad school(s), earning a Master's Degree, attending Churches, studying various religions and religious texts, getting baptized in several different churches, alcohol, countless self-help books, and more. I thought I had tried just about everything there is to try and was beginning to reconsider the idea that *I just need to get over it* and accept my life as it was. I thought, "I know what's wrong...I need to toughen up!"

The anxiety was always there though, no matter how productive I was or what I accomplished. It almost felt like a low level electrical current running through my nervous system at all times, and it was causing a consistent discomfort that was aggravating my whole existence.

Let me add something in regard to the timing of when I would feel the anxiety because I think it might be useful information: I could initially wake up in the morning, open my eyes in bed, and not really feel the anxiety for a moment. Sometimes, briefly, I felt just fine and relatively OK about the day ahead. But within minutes of thinking about getting out of bed, putting both feet on the ground, and facing the day, the anxiety would begin to slowly intensify. There was a sense of doom about what happened yesterday and then what might happen today, as if time was running out and I had to *solve the problem and win the game* before it's too late.

Then a new set of ideas on anxiety management came to pass as well, which also proved to be false.

Maybe I just don't have enough stuff yet?
Am I supposed to acquire more things, more degrees, more money?
Do I have the wrong house?
Wrong job?
Wrong neighborhood?

All. Wrong. Answers.

So if getting more and doing more isn't working, what would be the opposite of that?

Pausing here for effect...

Beginning to feel it yet?

Wait, is it possible that I am doing too much of something?

Wait for it...

The answer is YES, I was doing too much of something, alright. I was maintaining, holding onto, and trying to avoid something, all of which has been causing loads and loads of anxiety. And the energy required to maintain this false sense of holding everything together just to live up to a fake standard of living was fueling the negative cycle of anxiety I was stuck in.

You know what that false standard of living is? One where there is no pain.

*Even though I thought I was hiding or covering up certain things from my past that I didn't want to acknowledge, my behavior said otherwise. As a teacher, I now see behavior in my own students as a symptom and a means of communication.

Important note: I realize there is medication out there to help manage anxiety and I fully support anyone who is taking it.* For some reason, that path was not for me. If you don't finish reading this book, know this: I now have practically a zero level of anxiety (compared to what used to be anywhere from a 4-5) and I credit this change in anxiety to first acknowledging the fact that I experienced trauma and then accepting it, where as I thought I had to keep my true identity hidden.

*I am not a doctor, I am not claiming to be a medical advisor, and I am not saying to ignore your doctor's advice.

So rather than get more and do more, I started in a new direction - do less, get less, and take on less. That is when I realized it was time to give something up.

BIG QUESTION #1: What did I give up?

BIG ANSWER #1: The things that I was using to protect myself.

BIG QUESTION #2: What was I trying to protect myself from?

BIG ANSWER #2: The _potential_ of experiencing _that_ pain again.

We're going in deep here, buckle in.

As a child who was traumatized, something was taken from me - a sense of safety. That sense of safety that healthy parents provide for their children was not present on a consistent enough basis for me and as a result, left some long-lasting wounds. The feeling and fear of being powerless over bad situations are what ultimately kept the trauma alive, so to speak, which is also what lead me to the root cause of the anxiety.

But wait! There's more...

Let me put this another way. It wasn't the actual events in my childhood that caused my anxiety that I experienced as an adult, it was the fear of not being in control of something, or the feeling of being responsible for things that are not in my control, that were hidden under my radar of awareness or consciousness, thereby creating more anxiety.

I used to think it was a good thing to be totally self-aware and extremely hypervigilant. Even though I was often complimented on those characteristics (i.e. "you are very insightful, you are wise for your age, you are very self aware, you are an old soul"), inside I was like, "why can't I just chill the hell out and not pay so much attention to everyone and everything around me?"

It was Gary Zukav, one of my all time favorite authors, whose writings got me to see that I had a splintered personality along with a wounded soul that was in search of healing. That inner desire to heal came to me in the form of anxiety and when I stopped doing *all the things* that I would typically do to cope with that anxiety, I started to consider some key questions:

Did I cause this anxiety?
Did I create this anxiety?
If I couldn't **DO** anything in this moment, what would I do then?
What am I trying to control right now or avoid right now?

The QUESTIONS are what started opening up the path for me. It became more and more clear to me that I had to give some things up in order to heal. And the fear of giving those things up was also the same darn thing that would motivate me to glitch out and re-enter the negative cycle all over again. (see # 3 in the line graph below)

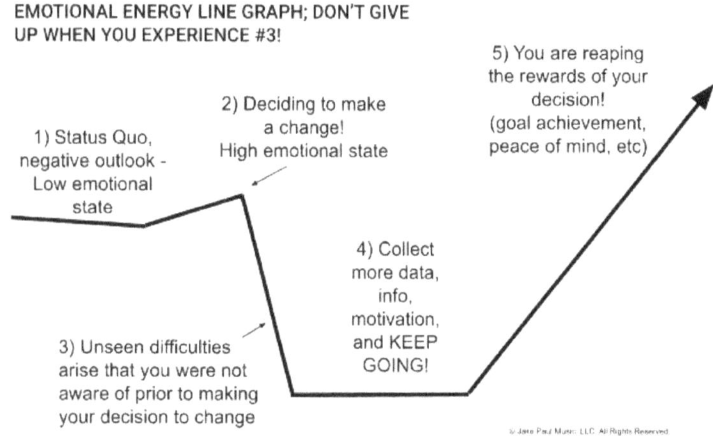

In order to take back what was taken from my childhood (a sense of safety and security) and complete this phase of healing, I had to realize a deep truth; **I didn't cause the trauma.** It wasn't my fault. *A child is not responsible for the adults in their life.* That realization opened up the next step on my path and I could sense that I was getting closer to the root cause of my anxiety. I saw that I was trying to win a losing battle of changing the past.

That's not all though. Since I am a master of disguise and a human chameleon (in terms of fitting in socially, also a trauma response), I even tried to trick my own self. For example, a part of me would say, "Ok fine, I get it - I didn't cause it. Can we go on now?" But my higher self recognized the defensiveness and emotional charge behind that urgency to "run away" and nudged me to **stay with those feelings** (which made me squirm inside a bit). Staying with those feelings means to not ***do the something*** I would normally do in moments of awkwardness or restlessness. So for me, I did the meditation thing, where I would sit quietly and ask myself those questions about the anxiety.

I WAS THEN LEAD TO MY DEEPEST WOUND - THE FEAR OF VULNER-ABILITY. I REALIZED THAT SITTING IN AWKWARDNESS OR DISCOM-FORT OR PAIN WAS...AWKWARD, UNCOMFORTABLE, AND PAINFUL. BUT BY NOT DOING THE *SOMETHING* I WOULD HAVE TYPICALLY DONE AT THAT MOMENT, I HAD TO ENDURE THE FEELINGS THAT I WOULD HAVE TYPICALLY AVOIDED AT ALL COSTS. IN OTHER WORDS, I UNCOVERED AND DISCOVERED THAT I WAS TRYING TO PROTECT MYSELF FROM FEELING VULNERABLE.

This is where recovery comes in to play. I "recovered" or found the pain I was hiding. **I had been trying to protect myself from it all along.** And I did a damn good job hiding it! But when I found it and realized that I didn't cause it (the painful event), I was able to accept it and let it go. And you know what happens when you let something go that you thought you were responsible for?

You feel relief again.

How did I let it go? I stopped trying to control it. Ironically and paradoxically, I gave it away. To whom or what? I am not sure, really. But it is no longer something I have to hide, manage, and maintain. It never was *mine* to begin with. I shared my story, broke the cycle, and now the anxiety is gone. I took the risk of being vulnerable again. I now feel safe again and I have forgiven the people who harmed me (which by the way, wasn't their fault either).

You can find other people who have also experienced trauma and you can share your story with them and they will share theirs with you and you can see that you are not alone after all. I am not trying to downplay your trauma, but it was helpful for me when I saw that my story wasn't *the exception to the rule* that I thought it was. You will also see that it is ok to be vulnerable again. That is a risk you'll have to take at some point in your healing journey.

I got to a place in my own healing process where I had to give up certain things that provided temporary pleasure and relief. Unfortunately, those things were also causing me (and my family) long term harm. They were taking energy away from me and keeping me in a low emotional state of being. For example, I gave up alcohol. In order to *follow the energy*, I saw that I had to put some things down for good that were taking my energy away. There are many difficult parts in making this choice, some I was aware of prior to making it and some I was not. But don't let that lead you astray, you must keep moving on with your journey.

* * *

Acceptance is the answer and the paragraphs I just wrote prior to this one are how I processed (worked through) the story from my past and as a result, the anxiety is gone. If you are dealing with anxiety, be hopeful. I was told that *it runs in our family* and *it is part of our DNA*. That is simply not true; the beliefs about it may run in the family culture, but the DNA part doesn't hold up. There is a better life out there ready for you to discover it.

The hero's journey is not any easy path to take...

...but in order to heal, it's the only path to take.

10

Synchronicities & Signs

What if there are no such things as coincidences?

It's easier now, of course, for me to talk about my life and how I followed the signs and found joy, peace, and purpose. It's easier too, for me to try and tell other people how to follow in my footsteps if they want to or are looking for a better way to view the world. I won't pretend that there isn't another reality though, where fear of making any real change is a very scary, perhaps even terrifying, thing to consider. I know it can hold a tight grip on anyone who even thinks about making the attempt to change for the better. As a general rule, be easy on yourself. When the time is right, you will in fact know it and you'll then take swift action.

When I decided to make a drastic change in my life, I [metaphorically] snuck out the back door. Being Irish, I figured I'd give 'em a real Irish Goodbye (Google it if you don't know what it means). I knew that if I announced *my big change* prior to doing it, not only would I have to face my own fears again but also the fears and insecurities of the people around me. I reminded myself that many people live in fear, have been taught to live that way, and are totally unaware that they are controlled (and owned) by it. That way of life does have an upside to it as well.

The downside, however, is that fear of actually listening to my inner voice or higher self kept me stagnant, in a negative place of discontentment, with a general dissatisfaction for what life had to offer. In plain terms, I could only find real peace of mind temporarily, if ever at all, and when I did it would often be followed by an extreme low. Although this book and my core message is that there is a wonderful life out there to be discovered, I recall very vividly what it feels like to be terrified of the unknown.

Staying put or living life as is might be more predictable and feel safer for a lot of people so I can see why so many people don't make a real, long-lasting change. If I could have found inner peace accepting my life as it was, I would have and none of these words would be here. To that point, I don't believe I had much of a choice in the matter as to whether or not I should make the leap and try to change.

I felt something deep inside of me calling me to take these actions and yet I was still too afraid to do anything about it. So I did what I think any rational person would do; I did what worked for me in the past. I started praying and asking for signs to help me know what to do. In regard to making a choice, my choices were this: live with pain, anxiety, and a general negative outlook on life or take a leap of faith and believe that there is more out there in store for us. I got incredibly lucky again - I saw signs.

I experienced miracles that I cannot explain or write off as mere coincidence and I found a sense of reassurance that I have a Guardian Angel or Angels guiding me along my way. Maybe you do too but like me, you have been rationalizing them as being just mere coincidence. Maybe if something happens once it is random. But if it keeps happening, it is time to pay closer attention.

A ghost-like spirit didn't appear in front of me and tell me what to do, but I did have an inner voice, if you will, nudging me to pray about stuff. So I started genuinely and sincerely praying.

When I say *sincerely and genuinely* I mean this: I stopped asking for what I thought I wanted (more money, bigger house, a better job, more time, nicer car, etc) and I realized I had been trying to negotiate for things as opposed to praying. In other words, I used to be like "Dear God, if you give me this, then I will do that more often and never do that other thing ever again." But now I started asking to be useful to others, for peace of mind, contentment, direction, and purpose. And I ended my prayers with "your will, not mine."

I went on with my normal life, which included an inner ping pong match between the realist and idealist in my head:

"What was I thinking? I just need to learn how to appreciate the good job I have. Yeah, I had a traumatic childhood but I need to get over it. I don't need to go publicizing it and making everyone think I'm a whiner and a complainer. Ditch the book idea, just do your job. Life is what it is, I need to accept that. Maybe ff I just earn more money and buy bigger and better things I'll be happy then. I can work harder at this."

...it was too late to go back, the signs began to appear...

Let me give a quick backstory to set this up for you. I have always been a fan of the number 4 for some peculiar reason - it has always been my favorite number, ever since I was a child. Paul Molitor was my favorite baseball player back in the day (Milwaukee Brewers infielder, number 4) and Brett Favre was my favorite football player (Green Bay Packers quarterback, also number 4). When people would ask what my favorite number is, number 4 just came to mind for some reason, not sure why. When the following *coincidences* started happening, I thought maybe I was just seeing what I wanted to see, like those psychological blotted ink tests I always heard about.

Then I woke up at couple days in a row at 4:44am...without an alarm being set. You ever try doing that on purpose? I sure didn't, I just woke up wide awake at that time. Why would I wake up right then? Why not 4:43 or 4:45?

On another instance while brushing my teeth I noticed the number 4 seemed to have been scratched in the drain plug at the bottom of my sink. "Interesting" I told myself because by this time, the number 4 had been showing up more frequently in my daily life. I took a picture of it (pictures on my website) and by now I was beginning to wonder why I kept seeing this number. Maybe there was more to it than random occurrence?

All within a couple weeks of one another, the signs were becoming too much to ignore. My receipt at a local cafe assigned me #444 (picture of it on my website) and I was having a moment of massive stress at school teaching middle schoolers how to cook when suddenly I looked at the stove clocks (the stove clocks were not accurate due to a power outage the night before) and all 6 ovens in my foods room had the time 4:44 flashing on them (again, pictures on my website)! My dart score two weeks in a row landed on 444 (pictures on my website). By the way, I am not that good at darts to be able to throw them intentionally enough to land on that exact score in the game 501.

* * *

There have been even more occurrences of the number 4, 44, and 444 in my life but I think you get the picture. So what does this all mean and how do I know that it means anything at all?

Choice. The dilemma is choice. We may *say* we want something, take freedom for example, but if that is true then the universe is going to call your bluff, so to speak, and see if that is in fact what you really are asking for. If you do in fact want to be free, doesn't that mean then that you have the freedom to choose whether to believe something or not to believe in something? If you choose to not believe in signs, what then are you hoping to see instead? What would it take to convince you to choose to pursue one path over another?

In my case, I asked for a sign, I started seeing number patterns, and I then chose to believe that something is guiding me along a path. I continue to see signs.

In my experience, all of this means that if you ask for help, or for guidance, or for a sign, then be sure to also do 2 other big things:

1) Get out of your own way! For example, I say "your will, not mine" in my morning meditation.

2) Look for the signs and synchronicities, clues, and other things that seem like coincidences and act on them.

Follow the energy and see where it leads you.

Part 3:

Verses of Victory

Crafting Songs in the
Light of Healing

As you read through these short stories and the songs that accompany them, you may notice a different undertone or theme in each story. By the time I wrote these songs, I either began to uncover and discover something that I'd been searching for practically my entire life, or I found pieces of *it* and started sharing my enthusiasm about it with the world.

Discovering that my life was not a prescripted, precasted, predetermined mold of doom can be compared to a paleontologist digging for fossils and discovering the world's most precious skeletal remains of a dinosaur. At first, I had to trust a hunch inside. *Where do I start digging?* For me it was like something inside of me was leading me to explore something more with my life. The synchronicities and miracles were my guiding compass. Next, I started digging. I learned to sit still, stop *doing* so much, and breathe properly, and insights began to surface within my thoughts that would give me a jolt of energy or excitement. By insights, I mean thoughts I had never thought of before, like new discoveries. Light bulbs were turning on inside. I was *waking up*.

Then, like the paleontologist, I'd dig even deeper and discover even larger fragments of the past. With each new discovery, the puzzle was beginning to come together clearer, and an overall lightness started to exude from my being. I could look people in the eye again. I didn't cower to the side of the hallways nor say "yes" to everyone who asked for something of me. I started building boundaries. I moved from pessimism to optimism.

These next chapters are about those discoveries, the messy work in between, and the songs that came out as a result.

11

Statue

*"Here I stand for you, no matter
what you've been through."*

The inner life of someone like me who experienced trauma was seldom at ease; my mind and body were always racing. The actual, physical, *non-action* of resting my body was very uncomfortable for me. I had to always do something, build something, fix something, write something, go somewhere, be somewhere, help someone, go get something, and so on. It wasn't until I discovered and uncovered my traumatic past that I realized I was still living with that trauma on a day to day basis and it was the driving force behind all of my *doing-ness*. If you would've asked me *why* I was so busy all the time, I'd have a legit or valid reason and explanation as there was in fact something I thought I had to do all of the time.

I realize that everyone has to get certain base-level things done in order to function on the daily and I also don't think there is anything inherently wrong with being busy, as long as there is a sense of balance as part of that equation. I was at a point though where I was never able to sit down and watch a show or read a fiction novel because I would get too restless about *all of the things I could be getting done* instead of just sitting around.

Now nobody truly has *nothing* to do; things do pop up which need attention, I get that. Like if something breaks and needs to be cleaned up, or if something needs to be fixed as quickly as possible then yes, a sense of urgency would be a normal response. That is not what I am referring to here though. I am referring to a constant inner feeling of needing to get something done all of the time, or that constant mental grind of always trying to solve some problem (one that usually didn't even exist in actuality) accompanied by a vibe of I *need to get this done today or else something bad is likely going to happen.*

SUBLIME is one of my favorite bands of all time. I'll use them to exemplify or to explain this condition. The next time you listen to the song, "What I Got" pay attention to the following lyric. Bradley Nowell writes, "got to find a reason, a reason things went wrong." That was my mantra on a daily basis and as I would get up in the morning my search would begin and wouldn't end until I went to sleep at night.

I often wondered, why do some people who don't seem to have that urgency to get as much done as possible all of the time still have so many things? I was perplexed by the idea that a person with more money than me, a nicer vehicle, and more "stuff" can sit down and watch TV, hang out with friends and socialize about anything they choose. They take breaks, naps, and do not feel the *need* I did to get everything done today. They didn't seem to have so many problems that demanded their *specialized expertise* to solve and they are able to talk about sports and weather without having to search for a psychoanalytical explanation about why the world is the way it is. The nature of their light conversations was always very intriguing to me. Not the actual content of the conversation, but the fact that they could have these talks for so long and seem to be content about it, without showing any real signs of anxiety about all the time they were wasting when they could be getting things done! Those people don't seem to be on the conveyor belt of endless searching that I was on.

So what was I really looking for with all of this doing, achieving, and busy work?

Well, I found it.

Stability. Safety. Consistency. Unconditional Love.

Sounds a little too heavy and part of me goes, "Damn, why do you have to get so deep about stuff all the time?" But that is what happens to someone who experienced trauma at a young age. And the truth is, that is what I was in fact always on the lookout for. So, I'm going with it and here is the lead into the next song, "Statue."

The song "Statue" is a letter I wrote to my future self about being there for someone no matter what. It may seem selfish to write a letter to myself, but then again, this entire book could be interpreted as being selfish, right? Consider this instead: if you knew of a small child who was living in an unstable and scary environment would you still call them selfish when they started to stand up for themself?

Of greater importance is knowing that just because people grow bigger and older doesn't mean they grow out of their childhood wounds. No wounds get healed until they are addressed. In a very simplistic way of explaining this - either you tend to your wounds, heal, and move on OR you repeat the same patterns over and over again, often times passing them on from one generation to the next until someone finally breaks the cycle!

Trauma isn't something people just grow out of when they get older - healing has to happen. This song was a turning point in my healing journey because it is when I began to see the qualities of the person I was searching for. It is when I realized that the sense of accomplishment I would get after checking everything off of my busy list is, deep down, giving me that sense of approval and acceptance I felt after getting so many things done. For the average reader, that may sound like a stretch to say that all of my busy-ness was really an attempt to not have to be busy, so that I could actually be present in the moment, accepted as I am, without always having to be looking out for something dangerous or scary. But look closer at the *why* behind someone who is always busy like that and you may see what I see is really hiding behind all of that work.

I planted a seed by writing that song and I am now seeing the fruits from it in my daily life. I want to scream it off the rooftops so that anyone who knows what I am talking about knows that it gets better! Further, the blame I used to use as a justification for always being busy and the anger I felt as a result of it has been replaced (mostly) with compassion. We are all doing the best we can with what we know. And when we know better, we do better.

Let's be here for each other, shall we?

Here I stand, for you.

"Statue"
© Jake Paul

Here I stand for you
No matter what you've been through
No matter what we gotta do
I'll always come through
For you

Here I am for you
There's not much I won't do
For You
When you're all alone
Can't find your way home
These words, these words
Are marked in stone
Like statue
Forever, like a statue

I'm walking through the pouring rain
Sometimes life can be a ball and chain
I hope you're in a better place
Cuz one man's loss
Can be another man's gain

Wondered if you'd still be my friend
If I put the poison away
Would you be there in the end
No matter what people say

Here I stand for you
No matter what you've been through
No matter what we gotta do
I'll always come through
For you

Here I am for you
There's not much I won't do
For You
When you're all alone
Can't find your way home
These words, these words
Are marked in stone
Like statue
Forever, like a statue

You never did see tomorrow
You only lived for today
How much time could you borrow
When did you intend to pay

I would still be your friend
If you put the poison away
Yes, I'll be here in the end
No matter what people say

Here I stand for you
No matter what you've been through
No matter what we gotta do
I'll always come through
For you

Here I am for you
There's not much I won't do
For You
When you're all alone
Can't find your way home
These words, these words
Are marked in stone
Like statue
Forever
like a statue

Go With The Flow

"It took too many years to realize

In a world made up of lies

We don't *control* anything."

It is astonishing to me to now consider how much time, energy, and resources I spent in the spirit of trying to control what I thought was *the way life is supposed to be.* To put it another way, not only did I think life was supposed to look and feel a certain way (for example, the image of the *American Dream*), I thought if my own life didn't match up to this preconceived ideal that I see on magazine covers, social media, TV, and in the movies, then I needed to double down on my efforts to try and control it to be more like what I see in the media.

Work harder, spend more hours at work, get it done faster, eliminate all errors and the people who cause them, and scale up the operation!

In one of my graduate level classes about the history of our educational system and how it was created, my professor opened us up to concept and creation of The Dominant Culture. Generally speaking, the DC is a set of beliefs created by a set or group of a certain type of people who are "in charge" of providing the information that the public in general has regular access to. In other words, have you ever thought about what information is provided to you on a daily basis (on TV, social media, newspapers) and how that information will make you feel once you receive it?

I got very curious about who creates the culture, and how it influences the masses to try and live according to it. Like George Carlin once said, "it's a big club, and you ain't in it." Guess what, no one is. It is an ideal created for people to try and live up to, and when they undoubtedly fall short, they feel like it was their fault. Hence the need for people to *believe* that they can control it and are responsible for building their lifestyle to match up to it. Also a big reason behind why most of the news is *bad news.*

Let me bounce back a little here - goals are great! Plans, ambition, motivation, and hope for a better future are mentally, socially, emotionally, and physically energizing! I say, go for it! What better reason is there to get out of bed in the morning than to work towards becoming the best version of yourself? Nothing wrong with trying to live your best life! But be sure you know what you are going for. Most of us can say we want a better or improved life, but few can explain what that means exactly. "Play the tape through" is one of my most helpful mantras because I once thought if I had something (say, more time) then I would be happy then. Then when I got more time, I was looking around at all of my time wondering what to do with it. You might see this sometimes (unfortunately) with retired people. They finally got *there*...only to see that there is not *here*. In other words, they fell for the trick that the future is where we need to be because *there* (not here) is where happiness and contentment are. Are you beginning to see how the trick is pulled over our eyes by the Dominant Culture? Play the tape through, what are you going to do when you get *there?*

> I hope you aren't missing too much here, spending all
> of your resources trying to get there.

So what is the solution? There isn't one. Well there might be actually, but I can't say what it is at this moment in time because I'm not looking to the future for a solution to a problem that doesn't exist yet. What I do know is that *going with the flow* means to be here, present. It means to be aware of what is happening around you and seeing how little control you actually have over it. It means, surfing on the waves on life's events instead of trying to get the water to calm down to your liking.

What causes your heart to beat? It's not you. What causes your hair to grow? It's not you. What causes your stomach to digest food? It's still not you. It's a total mystery in it's true sense because although there may be countless theories, philosophies, faiths, and belief systems to explain how your brain and body work, we really don't know what is keeping this thing called *life* going. So therefore there is no need to try so hard to control the outcome of the events in your life and the people who are part of it. I wonder how your attempt at controlling things is impacting those closest to you. The big lie I wrote about in the song "Go With The Flow" is in reference to the idea that we don't have any control in that sense of the word. Do we have influence though? Definitely.

"Go with the Flow"
© Jake Paul

I don't know who planned it
Or how we even landed
In this place again
It took too many years to realize
In a world made up of lies
We don't control anything

The moon fades away to sunrise
The tears trickle down from her eyes
She finally let'em all go
Never meant to hurt her
Never would desert her
We gotta go with the flow

Go with the flow
Let it all go
Go with the flow
Lct it all go
Go with the flow
Let it all go
Go with the flow

Who we gonna blame for this one?
There's no such as victims
Although it feels that way
Now she's in her front seat cryin'

While I'm desperately tryin'
To convince her to stay

Baby please believe me
Life is easy
When you ain't afraid to change
Take a look around you
At all the things that surround you
Nothin stays the same

Go with the flow
Let it all go
Go with the flow
Let it all go
Go with the flow
Let it all go
Go with the flow

Bridge
The pain is overrated
But the thought of us separated
Fogs me up with tears
The helplessness of attraction
Uncontrollable feelings of passion
Suffocated by fears

Go with the flow
Let it all go

13

My Side of the Street

"Soon I know the day will come
when I'm not afraid to love anyone."

As if love wasn't tricky enough as it is, imagine adding the element of not really having a true identity to the mix. I spent most of my younger life trying to be what the *dominant culture* told me I was supposed to be, but nowhere did it provide instructions on how to be true to myself, especially when it came to choosing a mate. As a result, I was constantly in a blind routine of guessing and checking, never really feeling confident that I knew what I was looking for in a partner.

After feeling frustrated and confused one night, I asked my grandpa at dinner how he found grandma and decided to marry her. Here is the wisdom he shared with me.

"Hey grandpa, how do you know when you find the right one to marry?"

"Oh you'll know" he said. "All of the other ones will fade away."

I was engaged at the time to a beautiful woman that *the world* told me I should marry. By all the admirable standards, she and I were a good couple. But I could sense that something wasn't quite right in terms of compatibility. I was too afraid and insecure to know any better so I suppressed my doubts and kept telling myself that things will get better with time. *Romantic relationships sometimes require work and effort to build.*

But one day while I was working as a teacher in a middle school I experienced what I can now say was love at first site. Of course, that is easy for me to say now, 20 years later, but going back to grandpa's advice, I knew right then at that moment when I saw her for the first time that she was the one for me.

The teaching staff was called to the library for a meeting after school and since I was a new teacher there I got to the library as quickly as possible in order to find a seat. I wanted to avoid the feeling of embarrassment of looking around for an open table in front of everyone.

I got into the library, set my things down at a table, when all of a sudden she walked in. This *glowing* woman walked across the room in a way that I can only describe as like "floating" past me. Time stood still for a second. I knew right then that there was no way I could follow through with my current engagement to be married after what I'd just experienced.

At first, I talked with my fiance and we delayed the wedding plans for six months. Eventually we called it off completely and went our separate ways.

The connection to trauma and recovery here is that I don't think I would have been open or receptive to that experience of meeting my true love if I'd kept numbing out my inner voice. Unresolved trauma can rob someone of those experiences.

* * *

Listening to my heart required taking a frightening leap of faith, but is also an essential part of recovering my true self.

"My Side of the Street"
©Jake Paul

These memories of you and me
And how happy we used to be
Now I see
That we agree
That we both want to be free

Caught up in circumstance
We had to take a chance
You just be
While I flee
Swim in the sea of destiny

Could you understand
This isn't what I planned
That doesn't mean I'm gonna lose hope
Can you comprehend
The messages that I send
I'm hanging from the end of my rope

But then she walked in
With a devilish grin
I knew today was gonna be the day
My new life begins
She had a flower in her hair
A sparkle in her eye
A smokin' little body with voluptuous thighs

She had that flame inside
Way too obvious to hide
We may crash and burn
But it would be a fun ride
She had sandals on her feet
I bet her kisses taste sweet
The sun began to shine on
My side of the street

So I grabbed another beer
And told her she should come here
If she wanted to have a good time
As soon as she got near though
Deep inside I feared, bro
I'd lose this girl to some other guy

But I believe in destiny
And if this was meant to be
Then nothin is gonna stand in my way, bruh.
So I did my best to trust
And hid my urge to lust
And listened to what she had to say, bruh.

She said, when I walked in
I saw your devilish grin
I knew today was gonna be the day
My new life begins
You got that sandy blonde hair
That sparkle in your eye

A fine physique
Way better than the other guys
You got flame inside
Way to obvious to hide
If we crash and burn
I bet it'd be a fun ride
You got those sandals on your feet
I bet your kisses taste sweet
The sun began to shine on
My side of the street

I never knew it could be this hard to let go
I still believe in love although I gotta take it nice and slow
Soon I know that day will come when
I'm not afraid to love anyone when
There's no longer a reason for me to run when
You and I are having so much fun
You and I are having too much fun!

That's cuz you came in
With a devilish grin
I knew today was gonna be the day
My new life begins
You got that flower in your hair
Sparkle in your eye
A smokin' little body with voluptuous thighs
You got that flame inside
Way too obvious to hide
We may crash and burn

But it'll be a fun ride
You got those sandals on your feet
And your kisses taste sweet
The sun began to shine on my side of the street

That's when the sun began to shine on
My side of the street

14

Inhale

"When I just took that last breath
I finally remembered that I'm always free."

At some point we've likely heard phrases like these:

"Actions speak louder than words."
"Talk is cheap."
"What you do matters more than what you say."
"Practice what you preach."
"Behavior is the true test of character."
"Words are meaningless without action."

If I were to ask you, "What do they all have in common?" the easy answer would likely be the overall theme, right? Something to the effect of *the actions you take are more important than the words you say.*

The irony is if I had to pin down the one action I took that helped me the most it would be to stop taking so much [meaningless] action! I would simply say **inhale before you exhale**. I'm being totally serious.

Reminding ourselves to inhale might be more valuable than you think. Here are a few reasons:

- it gives us time to think before we speak
- it gives us time to reflect on what was just done or said
- it gives us time and a reason to pause and think first
- it helps reduce the risk of a knee-jerk reaction
- it reduces stress and makes us chill the _______out
- it de-escalates a situation momentarily
- it provides oxygen to the brain
- it brings us back to the present moment
- it may provide a different perspective or interpretation of what you just experienced

The concept behind the song INHALE is the idea that you can only do what you can actually do in the moment and that is all there is to it. I know that falls short for those of you who might be wondering about specific strategies or methods of what to do exactly, but the truth of the matter is that you have to get rid of the blockage inside your head, so to speak, and that block-age is the direct result of what you are thinking in the moment. The desire or false belief that you have to control the outcome of things in order to get what you want (actually, what you *think* you want) often gets in the way of true resolution or any sense of real satisfaction.

To a very large extent, we have to *let it happen*. There were in fact events that occurred in our life that we had no control over and there are going to be many more in which we have no control over. I'm sure we all have things in our past that we wish we would have done differently but if you are picking up what I'm laying down here, I'm sharing a way of viewing the world that will lead you to a better mental and emotional state of being right here, right now. I am lighter and easier to be around now as a result of learning how to breathe without tensing up and holding my breath without even knowing it. I enjoy things now and I'm not trying to fix everything or everyone. I'm more balanced. I laugh more. I pay attention to what other people are saying more that I ever have in the past. I am "here" more often, rather than being a ghost or a shell of a person who appears to be here, but is mentally somewhere else.

Letting it happen does not mean to allow people to trample all over you. When I started to establish healthy boundaries, I then started doing what I needed to do in order to uphold them, and that was confusing to people who were not used to that. Even the people I am closest to were not always in favor of my *new* boundaries (nor do they have to be). And when someone gets mad or upset with me, I let that happen too. I let it play out, with as much kindness, consideration for others, and empathy as I can, knowing that if I bail out on my own boundaries we both suffer in the end. Instead, I try to stay centered in my own being, knowing that I am protecting my own self worth, my own mental and emotional health, and also doing what is best for the both me and you. I am being as real and authentic as I can be, and that doesn't mean other people have to approve of me. So I just relax for a minute and inhale. What's the alternative?

Hey let's try it!

1. Sit down in a position that is comfortable enough for you to stay put for about 3 minutes (to begin with).
2. While sitting there, tell your mind to focus on breathing in. Are you breathing out forcefully? Don't do that. Just inhale and tell yourself to surrender to the exhale. Let the exhale just happen.
3. Tell your mind to focus on breathing in again. Get out of your own way and let the exhale just happen.
4. If you notice yourself trying to stop doing this activity before the 3 minutes are up, take notice of yourself trying to control the situation again. What are you trying to avoid?*
5. Remind your mind to focus on the inhale.
6. Repeat until your time is up.

*If you are attempting to stop early because you are in a physically uncomfortable position, then get what you need to be comfortable and start over.

* * *

I'm not attempting to teach you meditation, this is just a breathing exercise that you can use throughout your day. I recall having sore trapezius muscles (in my shoulders) and a tense neck as a direct result of not breathing right. This is also what I mean by mental blockage and getting in your own way. I started applying it when interacting with people throughout the day and I have less tense, sore muscles. Again, I am *lighter, easier*, and less stressed as a result.

The alternative is to react first and apologize later. The alternative is to argue my point across until I think you understand me. The alternative is to be right. The alternative is to stress out over things and people for which I have no control over.

I wrote this song in the middle of an argument with someone very near and dear to me. I could sense that there was not going to be a "winner" at the end of this heated debate and I also recognized that I was getting pretty worked up trying to change someone else's point of view. So I walked away, went into my music room, picked up a pen and notebook, and began to write. I came out with the song, "Inhale."

"Inhale"
© Jake Paul

I forgot what I said
But will you remember to forgive me?
When all I saw was red
You were the one who encouraged me
When I was hanging on by a thread
You were the one who got me to believe
When I just took that last breath
I finally remembered that I'm always free
Oh yes I'm always free

To inhale
Before I exhale
You gotta give it if you think you want to take it
Or you ain't gonna make it
Very far with me
You gotta give it if you think you want to take it
Or you ain't gonna make it
Very far with me

Do you remember how it used to be
Everlasting feeling of joy listening to Sublime?
Together we could find Nirvana
Now we're chokin in our own drama so
Nevermind

They gave you everything you wished
You made a fist and a list
But forgot to add joyous and free
Take a look around ya
Tell me 'bout the good things you found
Since you've been runnin' with me

Let's inhale
Before we exhale
You gotta give it if you think you want to take it
Or you ain't gonna make it
Very far with me
You gotta give it if you think you want to take it
Or you ain't gonna make it
Very far with me

Bridge
So before we say goodbye
I always knew that we could make it
If we try
So wipe the tears from your eye
I always knew that we were gonna make it
If we try
Just inhale

You better inhale
Before you exhale
You gotta give it if you think you want to take it
Or you ain't gonna make it
Very far with me
You gotta give it if you think you want to take it
Or you ain't gonna make it
Very far with me

(outro/bridge)

JUST

IN...

HALE

15

Inclined

"If you want freedom,

open your mind."

Allan Cohen is the author and life coach behind *A Course in Miracles* (along with 30+ other inspirational books) and if you haven't experienced any of his work yet I highly recommend that you do! In his words, "Our history is not our destiny." That means that our past doesn't automatically determine our future, unless we want it to. For people like me, that is the gospel, or the good news!

History *is* a story though and once it is written it becomes information. What we do with that information is a whole different story. As a teacher who has been part of a curriculum renewal process in schools, I am aware of how some books and information make it into our schools while others do not. In summary, the books and resources are selected by a group of selected and/or elected people and when they are approved, they get added to the teacher's set of teaching materials. Have you ever wondered who, what, how, and/or why those books and information get approved while others do not?

At any rate, for the sake of this book, I'd like to point out that we all have a story about our own life. That story is like a movie that is constantly playing in our head. What is the theme of your movie? What is the plot line? Are there evil characters in it trying to get you? Is there a happy ending? Are you the leading role? Do you have enemies you are trying to defend against? Is there a major challenge you must overcome in order to be happy? Is there a hero?

> I was in Alaska hiking trails in Denali when I came to a unique realization: even though I was thousands of miles from home I still felt the same. I had a similar realization in Mexico as well. The point is that *no matter where I went, there I was.* I was under a false impression that in order to be a different person, I simply had to go to different places. It was then that I realized that my own mind is what is creating the experience and the feelings that come along with it. **The meaning of something didn't come to me, it came from me.**

When I learned this truth in my own life, I felt inclined to share it with those who might want to hear it. If you are looking for more time, money, and free choice in your life, I'm referring to you. If you feel restricted and painfully limited with your options in life, I am referring to you too. If you feel like this whole academic and economic system is beginning to sound like one big hoax, I'm definitely talking to you. Freedom must come from within first. But what the heck does that even mean, from *within?*

There are very poor people that are much happier than wealthy people. There are very overweight people that are more content than very fit people. I know someone who rides his bicycle everywhere and is much more joyous than the person I knew who was driving a top end Lexus luxury sports car. See where I'm going with this?

Let's flip it then just to make sure. There are very wealthy people who are much happier than very poor people. There are very fit people who are more content than very overweight people. I know someone who has an extra car in the garage and is much more satisfied with life as a result of having that car than someone I know of who rides his bike everywhere (especially when the weather is bad!).

It's not what you have or don't have, it's the meaning you place on your situation. I place a lot of meaning on my past - it has given me great strength and insight now. Without having experienced the trauma, I would not be authoring this book. Now that I have shared my story, I can put my past in the past. I know what serenity feels like. On most days, I've realized a very sacred truth: I already made it. I'm a success. There is no future that I need to work hard at now to get to later. I am here, now. I made it!

Some days I want more. Some days I want less. Overall though, I am grateful. I am lucky. I am content. I am free from my toxic addictions. I have opened my mind to the possibilities. I don't have all of the answers nor do I need to. Sometimes I'm a hypocrite and sometimes I'm spot on. I'm going to screw up at some point. I'm also going to kick ass. I'll fall short, and then get back up and try it again. You are going to beat me sometimes, but I'm going to enjoy watching you give your best effort in my presence. Thank you for giving me your attention, that is a gift too.

No matter what I see, say, or do, I still have a choice in the matter moving forward.

You now have a choice as well.

THAT IS WHAT IT MEANS TO BE
FREE FROM WITHIN.
SO WHAT ARE YOU GOING TO DO
WITH IT?

"Inclined"
© Jake Paul

"I climbed the trees
and I swam in the seas
Hiked the mountains up in Denali
I didn't know if I was ever gonna find

Finally then my answer came around
Now I'm inclined to share what I've found
FREEDOM COMES FROM YOUR MIND!

So if you want freedom
If you want freedom
If you want freedom
Open your mind

And if you want some freedom
If you want freedom
If you want freedom
You gotta open your mind

See I was born into a storm
Now it's time to perform
I'm not the norm, I don't conform
To the rules of this dorm
I know that everything will be just fine
As I sit back and relax and listen to Sublime

We're singing

If you want freedom
If you want freedom
If you want freedom
Open your mind

And if you want some freedom
If you want freedom
If you want freedom
You gotta open your mind

You ever wonder why people prefer
To struggle with life when things occur
Way out of our control, outside of our limit
Like their life is a game show and they're in it to win

You ever wonder why people desire
To control one another and pretend to be higher
That delusional mindset is the birth of a liar
Watch out for the smoke cuz there's bound to be fire!

FREEDOM! OPEN YOUR MIND!

Epilogue

This book is meant to be inspirational and hopefully transformational too. Even though I often hear that people cannot really change, I did in fact change and I broke a negative cycle that kept reoccuring in my life, causing more harm to the world than I cared to admit. If my words come off as preachy or "holier than thou," then I apologize and need to work on communicating in a more humble fashion. The heart of my message is a gospel - I have really good news to share with the world, especially for those who are still suffering! I searched for a long time for a solution to my anxiety problem and I finally found it. I am now healing instead of harming.

Not everyone wants to hear that message though and I know that there will be haters and doubters who will scoff at these lofty ideas. This book was way too long for them to read, lol. I also realize there are in fact people out there who would complain about winning the lottery. Some people are not interested in even trying to change and the reality of it all is that miserable people somehow are unable to look at their own involvement in the way their life turned out.

If only they knew the impact they have on their children and the people who care about them most.

We cannot let those attitudes derail us from living our best lives. There is too much to live for!

Healing is possible, miracles do exist, and life is good! I could and would not make up the story about the Bible flying open (from the Providence Chapter) although even I sometimes step back and say, "Wow, did that really happen?" If you choose to believe that it was *only the wind* that blew the book open to that specific page I think you may have missed the moral of the story. Miracles don't exist if people don't believe they exist, they are just coincidences. Or to put it another way, it really doesn't matter what or whom was responsible for that Bible blowing open to that specific page at that time - I **believed** it was a message from *beyond* and that belief changed the trajectory of my life, which is a miracle to me.

To cover my own legal bases, I need to say this: I am not a professional or licensed doctor, therapist, counselor, or anyone else responsible for your well-being. I am just a person who was burdened with doubt about where life was headed for me and whether or not I should even bother to pursue a better one. My instincts to keep moving and the coping strategies of writing songs, poems, and journals have worked for me to help me cope with and get through the painful situations put into my life. Then when I saw some real miracles occur that I would consider beyond coincidence, I gained just enough belief and enough hope to give something new a try. My hope is that this book and my message gives you enough belief and hope to try something new as well.

Each and every day I would take a small positive action and create something new. Whether it be writing a song lyric, a journal entry, creating a piece of art—or sometimes I just had to get outside and move, walk, or explore in order to create a new situation or a new scene. Some days the anxiety was so crippling I recall reminding myself to just breathe, walk, breathe, walk, breathe, walk. Now that anxiety I am referencing is totally gone and when I recall what it felt like, I can't help but spread the good news that it is not a permanent condition.

In closing, consider this idea for a moment:

> " Everything I never thought was possible for my life "
> has now become a reality.

I am legitimately baffled and in awe at how it could possibly be true that someone like me who was convinced that I was destined to a life of dead-ends and negative self-sabatoshing cycles, now has this life of options and possibilities. This is not about me bragging, this is about breaking out of cycles and discovering a whole new life that is exciting to live. For the doubters who are thinking, "But you wouldn't understand, my case is different." True, your case is different because you are not a clone of someone else. I thought I was an anomaly because I was so different than everyone else, and that my story is much worse than yours.

Keep in mind that the feeling of being so different is exactly what the doubter in you wants you to believe - that way you'll stay in isolation, or in other words, solitary confinement. That same doubt is what is preventing you from moving on and discovering your true self.

Which version of you do you want your family to remember? Which version of you do you like looking in the mirror at? Your lower self doesn't want you to go to a better place and leave it behind, it would rather you stay in fear and doubt. What it doesn't want you to know is that it doesn't really like your company either, it prefers to be alone. The best thing you can do for it then is to leave it behind. Chew on that one for a moment and then decide on what your next move is going to be.

I have one easy suggestion to get you started on a new path. Say this out loud: IT IS POSSIBLE. Period. Don't add any words to that statement like *if* or *when*. Just say it out loud and like a magic spell, things will begin to happen.

Now get up, breathe, move on, remember that there is no such thing as coincidences, look for the signs, follow the energy, and if you fall down, get back up and keep trying.

* * *

For more information and to stay connected visit:
www.jakepaulmusic.com

About the Author

While Jake's early years presented numerous obstacles, including family hardships and personal struggles, he refused to let these challenges define him. Instead, he turned to education as a means of empowerment, recognizing its transformative potential.

Jake's passion for music has always been a driving force behind the scenes in his life. As a singer-songwriter and performer, he captivates audiences with his soulful melodies and thought-provoking lyrics.

Beyond his achievements in music and education, Jake Paul's commitment to making a positive impact on the world is evident in everything he does. He is dedicated to nurturing the potential of every person who learns of his story, empowering them to overcome their own obstacles, self doubt, and to pursue their dreams. As an author, he shares his experiences and insights with candor and authenticity, inspiring others to embrace their own journeys with courage and conviction. Jake's story is a testament to the power of perseverance, creativity, and unwavering belief in oneself, serving as a source of inspiration for all who dare to dream.

More tools and resources at www.jakepaulmusic.com

Contact Info:

All fan mail should go to jake@jakepaulmusic.com

Instagram:
@jakepaulmusic

Facebook:
@jakepaulmusic

YouTube:
@jakepaulmusic444

9 798218 463885